The Spirit and Race in John's Gospel

The Spirit and Race in John's Gospel

Belonging and the People of God

RODOLFO GALVAN ESTRADA III

CASCADE *Books* • Eugene, Oregon

THE SPIRIT AND RACE IN JOHN'S GOSPEL
Belonging and the People of God

Copyright © 2025 Rodolfo Galvan Estrada III. All rights reserved. Except for brief quotations in critical publications or reviews, no part of this book may be reproduced in any manner without prior written permission from the publisher. Write: Permissions, Wipf and Stock Publishers, 199 W. 8th Ave., Suite 3, Eugene, OR 97401.

Cascade Books
An Imprint of Wipf and Stock Publishers
199 W. 8th Ave., Suite 3
Eugene, OR 97401

www.wipfandstock.com

PAPERBACK ISBN: 979-8-3852-3186-7
HARDCOVER ISBN: 979-8-3852-3187-4
EBOOK ISBN: 979-8-3852-3188-1

Cataloguing-in-Publication data:

Names: Estrada, Rodolfo Galvan, III [author].

Title: The Spirit and race in John's Gospel : belonging and the people of God / Rodolfo Galvan Estrada III.

Description: Eugene, OR: Cascade Books, 2025. | Includes bibliographical references.

Identifiers: ISBN 979-8-3852-3186-7 (paperback). | ISBN 979-8-3852-3187-4 (hardcover). | ISBN 979-8-3852-3188-1 (ebook).

Subjects: LCSH: Ethnicity in the Bible. | Race—Religious aspects—Chistianity. | Holy Spirit—Biblical teaching. | Bible.—John—Criticism, interpretation, etc.

Classification: BS2615.6 E78 2025 (paperback) | BS2615.6 (ebook)

06/02/25

All Scripture quotations, unless otherwise indicated, are my translations.

For my youngest daughter, Samantha. I am so grateful to God that I was given the chance to be your daddy. Thank you for spending countless hours with me in my office, especially as I write this book. You are my curly cutie forever! I love you.

Contents

Permissions		ix
Preface		xi
Bibliographic Abbreviations		xiii
1	Situating John's Gospel in Its Proper Context	1
2	Ancient Racial Ideologies	17
3	Marking One's Birth by the Spirit (John 3)	34
4	Accessing the Space of the Spirit (John 4)	49
5	New Disciples in the Diaspora (John 7)	63
6	The Family of God (John 13–16)	78
7	Harnessing Courage Through the Spirit (John 20)	93
8	Another Proposal for John's Pneumatology	106
Bibliography		117

Permissions

Scripture quotations marked CSB are from the Christian Standard Bible, copyright © 2017 by Holman Bible Publishers. Used by permission. All rights reserved.

Scripture quotations marked ESV are from the ESV® Bible (The Holy Bible, English Standard Version®), copyright © 2001 by Crossway, a publishing ministry of Good News Publishers. Used by permission. All rights reserved.

Scripture quotations marked NAB are from the New American Bible, revised edition, copyright © 2010 Confraternity of Christian Doctrine, Washington, DC, and are used by permission of the copyright owner. All rights reserved.

Scripture quotations marked NASB are from the (NASB®) New American Standard Bible®, copyright © 2020 by The Lockman Foundation. Used by permission. All rights reserved. lockman.org

Scripture quotations marked NET are from the New English Translation Bible® (https://netbible.com), copyright © 2019, used with permission from Biblical Studies Press, LLC. All rights reserved.

Scripture quotations marked NIV are from the Holy Bible, New International Version®, NIV®, copyright © 2011 by Biblica, Inc.® Used by permission of Zondervan. All rights reserved worldwide.

Scripture quotations marked NJB are from the New Jerusalem Bible, copyright © 1985 by Darton, Longman & Todd Ltd and Doubleday, a division of Bantam Doubleday Dell Publishing Group, Inc. Used by permission. All rights reserved.

Permissions

Scripture quotations marked NKJV are from the New King James Version, copyright © 1982 by Thomas Nelson, Inc. Used by permission. All rights reserved.

Scripture quotations marked NLT are from the Holy Bible, New Living Translation, copyright © 2015 by Tyndale House Foundation. Used by permission of Tyndale House Publishers, Carol Stream, Illinois 60188. All rights reserved.

Scripture quotations marked NRSV are from the New Revised Standard Version, copyright © 1989, Division of Christian Education of the National Council of the Churches of Christ in the United States of America. Used by permission. All rights reserved.

Preface

I HAVE WANTED TO write this book for a long time. Ever since I published my first monograph, *A Pneumatology of Race in the Gospel of John*, I noticed a desire among church leaders and parishioners for a more popular version of the book. *Pneumatology of Race* was my dissertation, written mainly for an academic committee. So, I always felt a little guilty when my students or church friends bought my book. I knew they wanted to learn about the role of the Holy Spirit and racial identity. My book was not the best work on the subject even though I had previously discovered a relative absence of the topic of race and ethnicity within the Gospel of John. In fact, I knew of only a few monographs that discussed race in John's Gospel, and we happened to publish our dissertations in the same year.

When I first wrote *A Pneumatology of Race*, I was living under the Trump administration when racial hostility toward migrants, Muslims, and Jewish people was at an all-time high. At the time of writing this book that is now in your hands, I am again thinking about race. I find myself in a similar situation with Mr. Trump, who is trying to become the next president of the United States. He has haunted American politics for the last eight years, and I am praying he will finally be exorcized at the ballot box in Jesus's name. Though I can never underestimate the power of white supremacy, fear of the immigrant, or demagoguery, I hope that things will be different. I sense that Americans are finally saying no to the politics of hate, fear, and division. In fact, I am also a bit more optimistic within my own field. Partly as a result of serious work done in classical studies, biblical scholars are taking another

Preface

look at the ancient world and the impact that racial ideologies had upon people's lives in ancient Greece and Rome. In other words, the reality of race is no longer viewed as an anachronistic idea applied to the New Testament. Since long ago, people have classified and understood differences among people groups. I hope this book can provide a more accessible reading of John's understanding of the Holy Spirit's involvement with race.

As alluded, this book is a popular revision of my earlier book *A Pneumatology of Race* (Pickwick). I try to summarize and keep the academic jargon to a minimum. Additionally, chapter 2 is an expanded version of "Race and Hermeneutics" from the *Handbook on Postconservative Theological Interpretation* (Cascade). This is a summary of my recent research on the ideologies of race and ethnicity in the ancient Greek and Roman world.

This monograph would not be possible without the editors and team at Wipf and Stock. I want to sincerely thank Michael Thomson for the many wonderful conversations at the Society for Pentecostal Studies. Your encouragement and interest really helped me get this project going. I also want to thank Lois Olena for your careful attention to the rough drafts of these chapters. I very much appreciate having someone look at the chapters and provide such excellent feedback and careful review. I also want to convey deep gratitude to my students at Vanguard University for their encouragement and kind words. This book also emerged because of a graduate class I was teaching on the Holy Spirit in the New Testament. It was then that I knew that a more sizable and popular monograph on the subject was needed.

Last, I want to express my appreciation to my family, especially my wife, Jessica Estrada. Though this book is particularly dedicated to my youngest daughter, Samantha, in reality, none of my work is possible without the aid, support, and love of my wife. Thank you for always working so hard to provide and take care of our family, especially when I sleep in after late nights of writing until 3:00 and 4:00 a.m.

Rodolfo Galvan Estrada III
Vanguard University, Costa Mesa, California

Bibliographic Abbreviations

AB	Anchor Bible
AcT	*Acta Theologica*
AGJU	Arbeiten zur Geschichte des antiken Judentums und des Urchristentums
AYBRL	Anchor Yale Bible Reference Library
BDAG	Danker, Frederick W., Walter Bauer, William F. Arndt, and F. Wilbur Gingrich. *Greek-English Lexicon of the New Testament and Other Early Christian Literature*. 3rd ed. Chicago: University of Chicago Press, 2000
Bib	*Biblica*
BibInt	Biblical Interpretation Series
HCS	Hellenistic Culture and Society
JBL	*Journal of Biblical Literature*
JSJ	*Journal for the Study of Judaism in the Persian, Hellenistic, and Roman Periods*
JSNTSup	Journal for the Study of the New Testament Supplement Series
JTS	*Journal of Theological Studies*
LCL	Loeb Classical Library
LNTS	The Library of New Testament Studies
NCB	New Century Bible

BIBLIOGRAPHIC ABBREVIATIONS

NICNT	New International Commentary on the New Testament
NovT	*Novum Testamentum*
NovTSup	Supplements to Novum Testamentum
NTL	New Testament Library
NTS	*New Testament Studies*
NTTS	New Testament Tools and Studies
R&T	*Religion and Theology*
RBS	Resources for Biblical Study
SNTSMS	Society for New Testament Studies Monograph Series
TDNT	*Theological Dictionary of the New Testament.* Edited by Gerhard Kittel and Gerhard Friedrich. Translated by Geoffrey W. Bromiley. 10 vols. Grand Rapids: Eerdmans, 1964–76
ThTo	*Theology Today*
TJ	*Trinity Journal*
WBC	Word Biblical Commentary

I

Situating John's Gospel in Its Proper Context

THE CHRISTIAN MOVEMENT IS a diverse and global movement with many different stories of origin, revivals, and leading figures. Though we are diverse, we are also united in that the Spirit binds us together and enables us to experience the presence of God. The ability to experience the intimate power and presence of God is something we all cherish. Though some Christian traditions may emphasize the dynamic role of the Spirit such as speaking in tongues, miracles, visions, empowerment for mission, prophecy, and healing, the Holy Spirit is not owned by any movement or denomination. We are all people of the Spirit in some way, holding the breath of God within our lives through either creation or conversion.

I experienced the power and presence of the Holy Spirit when I became a Christian, but to be honest, I had no idea that what Christians described as "Spirit baptism" was something I experienced during my conversion. Since then, the role of the Holy Spirit has intrigued me for a variety of reasons. Not only am I a member of the Pentecostal tradition, but I also find myself questioning, respecting, and appreciating this movement that became vitally important since the Azusa Street revival of 1906.¹ The Pentecostal tradition holds onto the belief that the same Spirit that occurred during the age of the apostles is presently active today and available for all people—empowering both women and men for service and ministry.

This book, however, is not a book on Pentecostal theology. In reality, Pentecostals traditionally emphasize the Gospel of Luke and Acts in their understanding of the Holy Spirit. This is, as Amos Yong describes, "not over and against Paul but alongside Paul (and the other New Testament authors)."² My focus in this book is the Gospel of John and John's understanding of the Holy Spirit. As a Pentecostal, I do not pretend that my own experiences or beliefs have no influence upon my interpretation. Nonetheless, I minimize these with much discipline. Instead, I approach this study of the Holy Spirit in John's Gospel as a cultural historian.³ That is, I want to look at the role of the Holy Spirit with a particular focus on John's cultural and social context. This does not mean I do not theologize within these chapters, but theology is not the primary concern. My goal is to understand how John's portrait of the Holy Spirit would have been interpreted for real flesh-and-blood readers living during the Roman Empire.

THE HOLY SPIRIT IN JOHN'S GOSPEL

Why such an interest in the role of the Holy Spirit in John's Gospel? If anything, the presentation of the Holy Spirit in John's Gospel is unique. Not only does John's Gospel include stories unlike the Synoptic Gospels, but the language and activity of the Holy Spirit are different. For example, the Synoptic Gospels do not use the word Paraclete (παράκλητος) and the phrase "Spirit of Truth" (πνεῦμα τῆς ἀληθείας) to describe the Holy Spirit. These are found only in John's Gospel. In fact, John's Gospel provides a portrait

1. A. Anderson, *Introduction to Pentecostalism*, 43; Espinosa, *William J. Seymour*, 7.

2. Yong, *Spirit Poured Out*, 54.

3. Estrada, "Contextualized Hermeneutic."

of the Holy Spirit that is distinguishable from the other Gospels but not too different that it should lead us to conclude that the Gospel is describing someone else entirely. The language for the Holy Spirit as "Paraclete" (παράκλητος) is found on four occasions within the Gospel (John 14:16, 26; 15:26; 16:7) and once in a letter (1 John 2:1). The phrase "Spirit of Truth" (πνεῦμα τῆς ἀληθείας) is described as being within and with the disciples (John 14:17; 15:26; 16:13) and compared to the "spirit of error" in John's letter (1 John 4:6). Again, these two expressions are not found in the Synoptic Gospels, including the Old Testament, yet they both hold a prominent role within John's Gospel.

When we compare the way that the Holy Spirit appears in the public ministry of Jesus, further differences become apparent. John's Gospel does not draw attention to the Spirit's involvement in Jesus's birth narrative as in the Synoptics (Matt 1:18–20; Luke 1:35). John begins his Gospel with a prologue absent of the Spirit's involvement, despite the strong allusion to Gen 1:1–2. Additionally, the Spirit does not lead Jesus throughout his ministry, nor does the Spirit come upon people.[4] In fact, there is no baptism of Jesus where the Spirit descends and identifies Jesus as God's Son. This story is found only in the Synoptics (Matt 3:13–17; Mark 1:9–11; Luke 3:21–22), and John's Gospel prefers to introduce Jesus with the Spirit already upon him (John 1:32–33). We also do not find any stories in John's Gospel that discuss the Holy Spirit being involved in exorcisms or healings.[5] Neither does Jesus provide any teachings that warn people not to blaspheme the Holy Spirit.[6]

Instead, the Spirit in John's Gospel concerns itself with topics on new birth, temple worship, the rejection of the flesh, and cross-cultural suspicion. The Spirit is also described as a Paraclete and discussed within the context of violence and the impending death of Jesus. Last, John includes a story of Jesus breathing the Holy Spirit upon the disciples while they were afraid and locked

---

4. Matt 4:1; Mark 1:12; Luke 1:17, 41, 67; 4:1, 14.

5. Matt 12:28, 43; Mark 1:23–26; 5:2, 8; 7:25; 9:17–25; Luke 4:33; 8:29; 9:39–42; 13:11.

6. Matt 12:31–32; Mark 3:29; Luke 12:10.

in a room. This reception of the Holy Spirit includes no Pentecost sermon by Peter, nor does anyone engage in speaking in tongues because of receiving the Spirit.

Perhaps this is the first time these differences have been brought to your attention. Striking as they may be, I do not want to propose that John's Gospel and the Synoptics are talking about two different Spirits. Not at all. This does lead us to wonder, however, what was going on and why John's Gospel has a different emphasis and teaching. When we really think about it, the portrayal of the Holy Spirit in John's Gospel needs explaining. Why does John's Gospel depart from the Synoptic Gospels and paint a new portrait of the Spirit in different contexts, including new descriptions of the Spirit as the Paraclete (παράκλητος) and Spirit of Truth (πνεῦμα τῆς ἀληθείας)? Did John simply have stories about Jesus's teaching that the other Gospel writers did not have access to? Or, more specifically, what were the situations, social circumstances, or controversies that could have motivated such a new perspective for the Spirit?

STORY OF THE SPIRIT IN SCHOLARSHIP

These questions have challenged scholars throughout the years and have been the focus of many studies on John's Gospel. For example, C. K. Barrett believes that John's Gospel stands closer to early Christian beliefs and piety.[7] He finds that one of the earliest challenges of the early Christians was the delay of the parousia, the second coming of Jesus. The solution to this problem was explained in terms of the Holy Spirit.[8] According to Barrett, the Spirit is the "eschatological continuum" in which the work of Christ is carried out, and the church is the proper sphere of the Spirit's activity.[9] Similarly, Raymond Brown claims that this view of the Spirit was needed for a community dealing with the deaths of the apostolic

---

7. Barrett, *St. John*, 74.
8. Barrett, *St. John*, 75–76; Barrett, "Holy Spirit," 1.
9. Barrett, *St. John*, 76–77.

eyewitnesses and the delay of Jesus's return.[10] This delay was causing many believers to lose their faith. Thus, the writer of John's Gospel used the concept of the Paraclete to justify the church's proclamation of the gospel.[11]

Another scholar, George Johnston, understands the situation a bit differently. He proposes that the community that received John's Gospel was dealing with some serious debates. Some within the community either elevated the role of John the Baptist, experienced synagogue excommunication, venerated Moses, or had docetic views of Jesus.[12] Johnston claims that the Spirit was articulated in order to stand in opposition to anyone seeking to displace the central role of Jesus with another spirit or intercessor such as an angel.[13] According to Johnston, confrontation and hostile theological views are the underlying influence of John's understanding of the Holy Spirit.

Gary Burge offers a new and different proposal. He claims that the evangelist reconstructed a traditional Jewish image within the Gospel for his own context, elevating the forensic metaphor and including the role of revelation.[14] Burge explores the Spirit in relation to other theological themes such as Christology, eschatology, sacramentalism, and witness. As he believes, the Spirit takes a prominent role in the anointing and indwelling of Jesus as the Messiah.[15] Since the Spirit was the seal that identified Jesus as the Messiah, this also meant that the Christians who received John's Gospel bore the mark of the Spirit, which affirmed their identity and authority in Christ as an anointed community.[16] Burge also believes that John is trying to correct the early Christians' understanding of the sacraments by helping them not take them so literally. He believes that this sacramental literalism or the

---

10. R. Brown, *Gospel According to John*, 2:1142–43.
11. R. Brown, *Community of Beloved Disciple*, 28.
12. Johnston, *Spirit-Paraclete*, 119–21.
13. Johnston, *Spirit-Paraclete*, 126.
14. Burge, *Anointed Community*, 31.
15. Burge, *Anointed Community*, 61.
16. Burge, *Anointed Community*, 175.

institutionalization of the church was not recognizing the presence and power of the Spirit.[17] Overall, Burge proposes that John's community was taught to carry on its mission in concert with the Spirit while confronting the hostile world through the power of the Spirit.[18]

Other recent scholars such as Craig Keener offer a refined approach to the study of the Spirit by detailing how it developed from a Jewish understanding.[19] Keener suggests that, historically, the Gospel is addressing a Jewish-Christian community both excluded from their local synagogue and facing pressure from Roman authorities to participate in the civic cult.[20] He asserts that the Holy Spirit functions as a major component of John's polemic against a synagogue leadership and a cessationist stream within Judaism.[21] He also observes that the Gospel's pneumatic language challenges Jewish purity rituals, proposes a spiritual proselyte baptism, and offers a new location for worship that transcends boundaries.[22]

Tricia Gates Brown, a scholar who utilizes a social-scientific perspective, insists that the cultural model of patron-client relations provides a useful analysis to understand the Holy Spirit, given that it illuminates the relationship between God, Jesus, the Spirit-Paraclete, and the Johannine community. Her analysis contends that the author and community can claim to know God because they have access to God's patronage through Jesus and the Spirit-Paraclete. The Paraclete, in this sense, can be understood as an abstract broker or mediator.[23] She thus interprets both Jesus and the Spirit-Paraclete as brokers or mediators for the Johannine community.[24]

---

17. Burge, *Anointed Community*, 170.
18. Burge, *Anointed Community*, 206.
19. Keener, *Spirit in the Gospels*, 1–26.
20. Keener, *Spirit in the Gospels*, 135.
21. Keener, *Spirit in the Gospels*, 26.
22. Keener, *Spirit in the Gospels*, 137–39, 151–60.
23. T. Brown, *Spirit in Writings of John*, 180, 201.
24. T. Brown, *Spirit in Writings of John*, 55.

Marianne Meye Thompson, however, challenges the assumption that the Spirit should be understood solely from a christological perspective. She points out that the Spirit is a distinct way of envisioning God's activity and presence in the world, which should lead us to understand the identity and character of God. Thompson contends that the essential role of the Spirit is to be a life giver and bring the presence of the Father and Son to a community in need of assurance.[25] Stephen Smalley suggests that the Johannine church was undergoing a growing conflict. Some who came from a Jewish-Christian background and had loyalty to Judaism were finding it difficult to believe in the divinity of Jesus. Others who came from a Hellenistic environment might have become uncomfortable with the claim that Jesus was fully human as well as uniquely related to God. As such, a unique portrait of the Holy Spirit was needed, given that disintegration of the Johannine community was becoming an ever-growing threat.[26] As he finds, John's portrayal of the Spirit is akin to his understanding of Jesus's identity.[27]

Certainly, many other scholars study the Holy Spirit, including Otto Betz,[28] Felix Porsch,[29] Andreas Köstenberger and Scott

---

25. Thompson, *God of the Gospel*, 145–83; Thompson, *John*, 318–22.

26. Smalley, "Paraclete," 289–92.

27. Smalley, "Paraclete," 292.

28. Betz draws from Qumran literature to suggests that one should understand the Spirit as an advocate in the legal sense. However, as he points out, the Paraclete does not function as an intercessor but a prophetic teacher who continues Jesus's revelation (*Paraklet*, 113–14, 117–214).

29. Porsch contends that the Paraclete sayings emerge from the conflict experiences of the church, yet he finds that the Spirit realizes Jesus's revelation and stands in place of Jesus (*Pneuma und Wort*, 322–24).

The Spirit in John's Gospel

Swain,[30] Craig Koester,[31] Max Turner,[32] and numerous others. What, then, is the point of reviewing all these scholarly views? Primarily, how one interprets the meaning and significance of the Holy Spirit often reflects how one interprets the context of John's Gospel. Although some do so more than others, there is the sense that the significance of the Spirit cannot emerge apart from an understanding of John's context. Those who explicitly incorporate the Gospel's context in their explanation of the Spirit gravitate toward specific circumstances, like the community dealing with liturgical issues, a polemical debate with false teachers, the death of founding leaders, or strife with the Jewish synagogue. One cannot escape noticing that a robust understanding of the Holy Spirit is difficult without some interaction with, or preliminary understanding of, the situation and period in which the Gospel was written.

Now, there is nothing wrong with this approach. Indeed, Wayne Meeks notices this issue when he states that John's Gospel is "unthinkable apart from a particular kind of religious community."[33] There are scholars such as J. Louis Martyn and Raymond Brown making hypothetical guesses on the possible scenario of the Gospel's primary readers.[34] Certainly, some scholars disagree with this approach, but we should not hesitate to presume

---

30. Köstenberger and Swain recognize that within Jesus's public ministry the Spirit largely resembles the Spirit's activity in the Synoptics. They argue that the fullest characterization of the Spirit is in the Farewell Discourse, which centers upon a missional understanding. See Köstenberger and Swain, *Father, Son, and Spirit*, 90–136; Köstenberger, *Theology of John's Gospel*, 393–400.

31. Koester observes that the Spirit relates to several fundamental issues such as evoking faith, disclosing the presence of the risen Christ and Father in the community, empowering the community to discern Jesus's identity, and bearing witness (*Word of Life*, 134–60).

32. Turner interprets the Spirit in the public ministry of Jesus as a Spirit of prophecy, which includes revelation, wisdom, and teaching. Ironically, when discussing the revelatory activity of the Paraclete in 16:13, he undercuts his claim by saying that revelation concerning future events does not apply (*Holy Spirit*, 57–88).

33. Meeks, "Man from Heaven," 76.

34. Martyn, *History and Theology*, 46; R. Brown, *Community of Beloved Disciple*, 41.

that the Gospel's teaching on the Holy Spirit can be enriched when the context of the readers is more accurately understood. These dynamics go together. The question now is, are there other potential realities other than theological, polemical, or liturgical?

RACE AS A HERMENEUTICAL LENS

This book is about the Holy Spirit, but it is not an ethereal interpretation of the Holy Spirit unconnected to the living realities of people in the ancient world. Primarily, though, I argue that the theology of the Holy Spirit in John's Gospel reflects a context that understood the importance of people's racial identity. I explain in the following chapter what I mean by "race" and "ethnicity" and how this language is not anachronistic. Before I do, though, it is important to recognize that the notion of race or ethnicity, including hostile race relations, is not something limited to our contemporary era—these realities also existed within the context of emerging Christianity.[35] In fact, it was the early Greeks who invented the notion of otherness when they first started to call the Persians "barbarians." For this reason, I interpret John's portrayal of the Holy Spirit in light of the racial ideologies, prejudices, challenges, and stereotypes that were part of the Roman Empire.

Now, it is possible that much racial suspicion and tension from the wider Greco-Roman world made it difficult for the believers in John's community to understand their place within the newly formed family of God. Perhaps many of these members still held onto racial hostilities toward their Jewish brethren. Others, just maybe, experienced prejudice and phobias from them. If this were the case, which it might be, this also means that John felt compelled to articulate a new understanding of the Holy Spirit that would enable the believers to embrace and develop a new understanding of themselves and their place within the emerging Christian community. Racial tensions have been and still are

---

35. Sherwin-White, *Racial Prejudice*, 1; Isaac, *Invention of Racism*, 1–5; Buell, *Why This New Race*, 1–34; Buell, "Challenges and Strategies"; Horrell, "Race, Nation, People"; McCoskey, *Race*, 1–34; Schäfer, *Judeophobia*, 6.

ongoing problems—and the Christian community is not exempt from this challenge. This does not assume that every single teaching about the Holy Spirit has some racial implication but that a racial thread does connect many of these passages.

In a sense, I am also proposing that we not only become focused upon a Spirit Christology (that is, understanding the Holy Spirit solely in light of Jesus's identity) but that we also recognize that the Gospel is articulating an understanding of the Spirit that shapes people's understanding of race—a racial pneumatology, so to speak.[36] Said differently, the Gospel provides the grounds for thinking and exploring the significance of the Holy Spirit that interacts and concerns itself with the living experiences of racial identity, racial lives, and racial communities. Without such insights on the racial ideologies and experiences of people in the ancient Roman world, our analysis of the Spirit will fail to touch the real flesh-and-blood issues surrounding the context of emerging Johannine Christianity.

SITUATING JOHN'S GOSPEL WITHIN EARLY CHRISTIANITY

Now, I also want to briefly situate John's Gospel within early Christianity with some background information on the author, date, location, and readers. You will notice that I do not depart much from the traditional arguments. Nonetheless, here is the rationale for the perspectives assumed throughout this book.

Traditionally, the Gospel has been claimed as written by John the apostle. Many early church fathers overwhelmingly affirm the writer as John, one of Jesus's twelve disciples. In the second century, Irenaeus confirmed that John the apostle wrote the Gospel while he was staying in Ephesus. He states, "John, the disciple of the Lord, who also had leaned upon His breast, did himself publish a Gospel during his residence at Ephesus in Asia."[37] Irenaeus's tes-

---

36. Estrada, *Pneumatology of Race*, 292–97.
37. Irenaeus of Lyons, *Adversus haereses* 3.1.1.

timony is not alone. Other early church fathers such as Tertullian, Clement of Alexandria, Dionysius of Alexandria, and Jerome also affirm John the apostle as the author of the Gospel.[38] Thus, overall, we can notice that the early church believed that the apostle wrote the Gospel of John.[39]

Although the early church testimony presents strong evidence for John's authorship, how reliable are these perspectives? Critical scholarship has taken a closer look at the Gospel itself and has raised doubts. In fact, nowhere in the Gospel does the name "John" appear in reference to the disciple. Instead, the Gospel claims to be dependent upon the "one whom Jesus loved," also known as the beloved disciple. Who is this mysterious person known as the "beloved disciple"? Is the beloved disciple actually John the apostle himself, another person, or a symbolic figure as Rudolf Bultmann proposes?[40] In my opinion, no other person from the twelve apostles seems to match this unnamed character but John the apostle,[41] but this is certainly not a solid, clear-cut case.

There are, however, portions within the Gospel where the verses admit that another writer or group of writers was involved in its composition.[42] However, not all scholars are sure that these verses really indicate anything.[43] Traditionally, the early church fathers believed that the author of the Gospel was John the apostle, and I concur with their perspective. This, however, does not mean

---

38. Tertullian, *Marc.* 4.2; Eusebius, *Hist. eccl.* 6.14.7; 7.25.7; Jerome, *Vir. ill.* 9. The Muratorian Canon, a fourth-century fragment that lists books of the New Testament, indicates that John the apostle was encouraged by his disciples to write his account of the gospel. It concludes by noting that John was "not only an eyewitness and hearer, but also a writer of all the marvelous deeds of the Lord." Eusebius includes the gospel among his list of accepted writings and affirms that John the apostle was the author (*Hist. eccl.* 3.25.1).

39. Eusebius, *Hist. eccl.* 3.24.7.

40. Bultmann, *Gospel of John*, 484–85.

41. By the fourth century, Jerome, a Latin church father, affirmed that John the apostle was the one whom Jesus most loved (*Vir. ill.* 9).

42. See John 19:25–27, 35; 21:20–25; and Ray Alan Culpepper's explanation (*Anatomy of Fourth Gospel*, 44–48).

43. Keener, *Gospel of John*, 112; Morris, *Gospel According to John*, 726.

the apostle actually penned every single word and received no help in writing the Gospel's final form.

I also follow the traditional location of John's Gospel.[44] The Gospel has a particular polemic against John the Baptist, a tone not reflected in the Synoptic Gospels but one that reflects an Ephesian community's awareness of John the Baptist's disciples as noted in Acts 19:1–7.[45] Second, the Gospel also reflects an incipient anti-docetic and anti-gnostic polemic associated with the city of Ephesus.[46] This fits with Irenaeus's claim that the Gospel was written in Ephesus to refute the teachings of Cerinthus, a follower of Nicolaitan.[47] Third, the Gospel's anti-synagogue motif in John (9:22; 12:42; 16:2) also fits with the issues that Apollo and Paul had in the synagogue as noted in Acts (18:24–28; 19:8–10) and the whole Asian region.[48] Furthermore, the Gospel might have been written with Samaritans in mind, especially since they traveled beyond their region and were located on the Greek island of Delos, 150 miles from Ephesus.[49] Last, the Gospel's plot revolves around Jerusalem, which would have resonated largely with an Ephesian urban reader.[50] Both Jerusalem and Ephesus were known as temple cities.[51] Certainly, we cannot be sure of the Gospel's exact location of composition. True, Ephesus reflects various characteristics common to many Hellenistic cities, and we do know that John the apostle was known to have resided and been buried in this city.[52]

---

44. Eusebius, *Hist. eccl.* 3.20.11; 3.23.4–3.23.7; 3.39.1–3.39.7; 5.24.3.

45. John 1:8, 24; 3:30; Marcus, "Johannine Christians"; R. Brown, *Introduction*, 156.

46. R. Brown, *Introduction*, 124, 205.

47. Irenaeus of Lyons, *Adversus haereses* 3.11.1.

48. Keener, *Gospel of John*, 148.

49. R. Anderson and Giles, *Keepers*, 29–30.

50. Van Tilborg, *Reading John in Ephesus*, 63.

51. Van Tilborg, *Reading John in Ephesus*, 69–74.

52. Eusebius, *Hist. eccl.* 5.24.3; Jerome, *Vir. ill.* 45. John the apostle would have been another towering figure in this city, along with others such as Apollo, Paul, and Timothy (Acts 18:19–21, 24–28; 19:1–20; Eph 1:1; 1 Tim 1:3; Rev 2:1–7).

Situating John's Gospel in Its Proper Context

Church tradition has always associated the Gospel with Ephesus, and no valid reason exists for dismissing this claim.

Church tradition also affirms that the Gospel was written after the Synoptics. Many church fathers notice the differences among the Gospels and try to explain their relation, believing that John's Gospel was written to supplement what was lacking in the Synoptics.[53] Though scholars do not believe in this supplemental theory, we are certain that the Gospel could not have been written later than the second century. One of the oldest fragments of the New Testament is the John Rylands Manuscript (P52), which includes John 18:31–33 and 37–38. This manuscript is dated between 100–150 CE.[54] Its existence within the second century demonstrates that the Gospel was already circulated as far south as Egypt.[55] This leads us to reliably conclude that the Gospel was written anytime in the late first century between 60 and 100 CE.

Now that we have established the author, location, and date, the next aspect to explore is the context of the Gospel. When we think about early Christianity in the late first century, this was a period in which there was a gradual separation between Jews and Jewish Christians. Strikingly, this tension permeates the Gospel with its description of synagogue excommunication and the portrayal of Jesus's experiences with his own Jewish people. It was Martyn who proposed the thesis that the Gospel was written for expelled Jewish Christians who had had a hostile experience with the synagogue.[56] Raymond Brown builds from this premise to include Samaritans and some Greeks.[57] Scholars recognize that the Gospel not only narrates the story of Jesus but does so with the story of the Johannine community in mind.[58] The identity of the readers, also known as the Johannine community, has been vigorously debated in scholarship. Views range from those who argue

---

53. Smith, *John Among the Gospels*, 6–8; Eusebius, *Hist. eccl.* 3.24.7; 6.25.6.
54. Metzger, *Text of New Testament*, 38–39.
55. Metzger, *Text of New Testament*, 39.
56. Martyn, *History and Theology*, 61.
57. R. Brown, *Community of Beloved Disciple*, 55–59.
58. Skinner, *Reading John*, 32–46.

that the primary readers were expelled Jews to those who propose a much broader audience.[59] In fact, Richard Bauckham writes that the "author deliberately made his work accessible enough to outsiders for it to be read with profit by nonbelievers, Jewish or Gentile, who might be introduced to it by Christian friends."[60]

Now, the claim that John's Gospel was written for a universal audience does not necessitate abandoning questions about the context of the community or the racial identity of the readers. A universal audience makes it even more necessary to pay close attention to the representation, portrayal, engagement, and manner in which various people within the Gospel emerge. One cannot fail to recognize that the Gospel itself has a special interest in recording various encounters with people from diverse racial backgrounds. For instance, when Jesus journeys to Jerusalem, he meets an unnamed Samaritan woman and spends many days with the people of Samaria (John 4:2–42). This story of Jesus being with Samaritans and spending several days in the region is found only in John's Gospel. Furthermore, during one of Jesus's teachings in Jerusalem, Jesus is accused of desiring to leave the region and travel to the Greeks in the diaspora (7:35). This story is often read as an accusation that he is going to visit Hellenistic Jews, but much later in the Gospel there is a story of Greeks coming to the disciples and petitioning a personal meeting with Jesus (12:20–26). Only John's Gospel records such Greek interest in Jesus and the suspicion that Jesus is going to find disciples among the Greeks.

Still, Samaritans and Greeks are not the only referenced characters in the Gospel. When the Pharisees recognize Jesus's miraculous activity attracting too much attention, they realize that something needs to be done to prevent a Roman intervention (John 11:48). They suppose that Jesus's popularity could lead to Roman suppression and expulsion from the land. This conversation between the religious leaders is a unique story found only in John's Gospel. We do not find such fear of possible violence or uprooting

---

59. Culpepper, *Anatomy of Fourth Gospel*, 218; Bauckham, *Gospels for All Christians*, 1–11.

60. Bauckham, *Testimony of Beloved Disciple*, 13.

Situating John's Gospel in Its Proper Context

of the Jewish people from their land in the Synoptic Gospels (Matt 24:15–16; Mark 13:14–15; Luke 21:24). Last, only John's Gospel includes a dialogue between Jesus and Pilate that makes mention of Jesus's racial identity. Pilate, in fact, puts the reality of Jesus's racial identity to the forefront when he asks, "Am I a Jew?" (John 18:35). No such discussion or mention of racial identity during Jesus's dialogue with Pilate appears in the Synoptics.

Why does John's Gospel mention all these various characters within the story that strikingly differs from the Synoptic Gospels? It may be quite possible that John does so to highlight the fact that Jesus's story is also the reader's story. Since John's community was a multiracial community, the Gospel is written in such a way that it represents the identity of the Gospel's diverse readers. We can notice John's sensitivity to his readers when he translates various Jewish terms[61] and customs.[62] This is also perhaps why the Gospel demonstrates some affinities with non-Christian thought. The Gospel reflects an ability to communicate to both Jewish and non-Jewish readers—and everyone in between. The Gospel's audience was not a neutral, nonracial universal audience—it was a multiracial community that needed to hear the story of Jesus in their own words. Fortunately, John not only writes with a multiracial community in mind but also narrates Jesus's multiracial ministry.

SURVEY OF THE JOURNEY AHEAD

As a result of the Gospel's multiracial context and unique portrayal of the Holy Spirit, this book proposes a new way of demonstrating how these two elements relate. For this reason, in chapter 2, I explain what I mean by "race." This includes more specifically how the ancient Greeks and Romans thought about race and how people groups were classified. In the following chapters, we incorporate this background into our interpretation of John's teaching on the Holy Spirit.

---

61. John 1:38, 41–42; 4:25; 9:7; 11:16; 19:13, 17; 20:16.
62. John 2:6; 4:9; 10:22; 18:28; 19:40.

Chapter 3 thus discusses the conversation between Jesus and Nicodemus on the topic of being born again by the Spirit. Chapter 4 discusses the role of the Spirit in Jesus's discussion with the unnamed Samaritan woman. Chapter 5 explains how Jesus's teaching on the Spirit make sense in light of the suspicion that he was going to leave to teach the Greeks. Chapter 6 focuses on the significance of the Paraclete in light of Jesus's kinship language. Chapter 7 focuses on the post-resurrection appearance of Jesus and when the Holy Spirit is given to the disciples. The final chapter proposes a theology of the Holy Spirit with a particular focus on what it means to belong to the family of God.

Though I do not provide analysis of every mention of the Spirit in John's Gospel, this book does highlight some of the important chapters vital for our understanding of John's theology.[63] My hope, overall, is that this book will provide a new way of thinking about John's view of the Holy Spirit, including the way in which the Holy Spirit continues to bind us together as the people of God.

---

63. For a more detailed study, see Estrada, *Pneumatology of Race*.

2

Ancient Racial Ideologies

WE MAY PRESUME THAT the terms for "race" or "ethnicity" emerged after the colonization of the Americas or when scientists of the eighteenth and nineteenth century began to classify people into different groups. Applying the concept of "race" to our study of John's Gospel is not an anachronistic move, nor is it a new concept to those in the ancient world—it has been around for a long time. When we look at how people groups were defined in ancient Greece and Rome, we see that a host of matrixes defined racial and ethnic identity, such as clothing, food, religion, language, lineage, laws, and geographical origins. This does not presume that the development of a racial conscience did not emerge in the Old Testament,[1] although it is difficult to understand the role of race and ethnicity in pre-monarchical Israel.[2] But within the New Testament world, the influence of Greek and Roman thought is noticeable.

It was Herodotus, a historian of ancient Greece, who records a speech by the Athenians to the Spartan envoy that explains why the Athenians did not join the Persians to enslave the Greeks. They appeal to common identity markers and point to the "kinship of all

---

1. The Old Testament includes many passages on "foreigners" who lived among the Israelites, although Rendtorff mentions that the identities of these people are difficult to identify ("*Gēr* in the Priestly Laws").

2. Edelman, "Ethnicity and Early Israel."

Greeks in blood and speech, and the shrines of gods and the sacrifices that we have in common, and the likeness of our way of life."[3] Notice how aspects of Greek identity within this quote include a common descent, language, religious observance, and way of life. Much later, Isocrates provides a cultural understanding of race and its relationship to the Greek intellectual heritage. He states, "Hellenes suggests no longer a race [γένους] but an intelligence and that the title Hellenes is applied rather to those who share our culture than to those who share a common blood."[4] In Roman literature, these aspects and others were signs of racial identity. Virgil describes the diversity of the human race based upon the diversity of their clothing, weaponry, and language (*Aen.* 8.720). Likewise, Tacitus also describes the racial transformation of the Britons to a Roman identity when they started to adopt Roman customs, education, clothes, and food (*Agr.* 21.1).

Overall, the ancients used the Greek terms γένος (race), ἔθνος (ethnic), and λαός (people) to describe themselves, distinguish others, identify their descendants, or address people groups in general. Although Eric Gruen admits that the term "race" may be a misleading and erroneous category, given its modern usage,[5] it is thus helpful to think about race as classification language that organizes human difference. The idea of race appears whenever the ancients attempt to distinguish people groups from one another and also set the boundaries between themselves and others.[6] Specifically, as "us-them" language, it emerges specifically whenever people feel they need to emphasize group identity or indicate some sort of difference between groups. This is also why conversations about race emerge more frequently when people from different racial backgrounds come together, in comparison to those who live in a homogeneous community.

---

3. Herodotus, *Persian Wars* 8.144.
4. Isocrates, *Paneg.* 50.
5. Gruen, *Rethinking the Other*, 197–98.
6. McCoskey, *Race*, 2; Estrada, *Latino Reading of Race*, 17.

In the New Testament, the term "race" is a translation of the Greek word γένος.[7] This term (γένος) appears only twenty times in the New Testament, with almost half found in Acts (nine occurrences). The term highlights distinct people groups such as the Syrophoenician woman, gentiles, Jewish people, and Christians.[8] Generally, "race" is used for descendants, family, or association with land.[9] Love Sechrest, in fact, notices that this term refers to people groups, language, kinship, humanity, territory, customs, government, war, and a founding figure.[10] Similarly, Denise Buell aptly suggests that the common use of the term "race" would have signaled a group classification.[11] She insists that it demarcates a group whose membership would share certain characteristics such as ancestors, rights of inheritance, knowledge, ritual practice, and ways of life.[12] This broad application should lead us to recognize that race is primary classification language, as Buell insists.

But what about the word "ethnicity"? The term "ethnicity" (ἔθνος) is also used to describe people groups. It appears more frequently in comparison to γένος, appearing 162 times, with most occurrences in Acts. This is a popular term used for gentiles, especially in the Pauline Letters[13] and Revelation.[14] However, ἔθνος is used in reference to the Jews in the Gospel of John.[15] These diverse uses demonstrate the notion of "ethnicity" as something observable, applied to distinct groups of people, and reflective of an acknowledgment of group difference. In fact, John Balsdon finds that

---

7. The term refers to posterity, family, people, kind, or species. See Friedrich Büchsel, "γένος," *TDNT* 1:685–90.

8. Mark 7:26; 2 Cor 11:26; Phil 3:5; 1 Pet 2:9.

9. Acts 4:6, 36; 7:13, 19; 13:26; 17:28–29; 18:2, 24; Rev 22:16.

10. Sechrest, *Former Jew*, 81–90.

11. Buell, *Why This New Race*, 1.

12. Buell, *Why This New Race*, 2.

13. Rom 1:13; 1 Cor 1:23; Gal 1:16; Eph 2:11; Col 1:27; 1 Thess 2:16; 1 Pet 2:12; 4:3.

14. Rev 5:9; 7:9; 10:11; 12:5; 14:6–8; 15:4; 16:19; 17:15; 18:3, 23; 19:15; 20:3, 8; 21:24, 26; 22:2.

15. John 11:48, 50–52; 18:35.

the Jews divided humanity into Jews and gentiles (ἔθνος) just as the Greeks divided humanity into Greeks and barbarians.[16]

The classicist Benjamin Isaac defines "ethnic group" as a people who share a long history, beliefs, traditions, distinguishable characteristics, and a cultural tradition of their own, including family, social customs, and manners.[17] Jonathan Hall notices that within ancient Greece, ethnicity was not solely a biological phenomenon but developed in opposition to other ethnic groups.[18] As Hall believes, it was the war with the Persians in 480–479 BCE that compelled the Greeks to define themselves as an ethnic group.

Although "race" and "ethnicity" are difficult to precisely define and are used synonymously throughout the biblical and contemporary era, it makes sense when people today use them interchangeably. There is a historical reason, though, why we use these terms today—partly the result of the UNESCO statements on race when the world's scientists sought to make an international declaration condemning the racial ideologies that led to World War II. These international scientists responded to the pseudo-science and myths of race that defined race in biological terms, differentiated different species of humanity, and claimed that race mixture was harmful to humanity. The UNESCO statement encouraged the use of "ethnic groups" since the term "race" contains serious errors in popular thinking.[19] Unfortunately, though, the use of the term "race" has not fallen out of use as hoped, and both terms are used interchangeably.

Given the contemporary use of the terms, their history, the potential for misunderstanding, and similar definitions, should we reject this language altogether? Certainly not. In fact, Buell argues that although "race" and "ethnicity" are modern categories, we cannot assume they were irrelevant to early Christians. She notices that early Christian strategies of self-definition resonated with both ancient interpretations of cultural difference and

16. Balsdon, *Romans and Aliens*, 234.
17. Isaac, *Invention of Racism*, 35.
18. J. Hall, *Ethnic Identity*, 33.
19. UNESCO, "Scientific Basis," 8; Rahim et al., "UNESCO Statement."

modern ones.[20] What is most important is recognizing how we use the terms "race" and "ethnicity" to identify boundaries between people groups. People groups share distinct identity markers such as culture, lineage, religion, territory, clothing, food, language, and myths of descent, to name a few. These boundaries, however, are not permanent but always shifting and negotiated by both members and nonmembers of the group.

As a result, we must be disabused of the notion that "race" or "ethnicity" are permanent, scientifically rooted in biology, and associated with skin color. This is not how the ancients thought about race. Simply because they did not associate race with skin color or biology does not mean they had no understanding of the idea. They identified differences—whether cultural, religious, territorial, or myths of descent—but these differences were not impenetrable boundaries. Instead, their view of race and ethnicity was much broader and negotiable. They could identify and classify different people groups, and knowing that racial identity was malleable, the fear of losing one's racial identity also existed if one did not remain vigilant regarding group boundaries.

RACIAL IDEOLOGIES: ENVIRONMENT, GENEALOGY, AND CULTURE

One of the challenges we have in identifying race in the New Testament is that we do not think about race as those in the biblical world did. Observable phenotypes such as skin color and bodily features help us make sense of racial groups. We see blond hair, and North American or European racial groups come to mind. We see brown skin with almond eyes, and Latin American or indigenous races are a likely guess. This way of thinking is ingrained within our society.

Color is a racial signifier in our modern world. We use color language to distinguish people groups. Those who lived in the ancient world would have found this way of defining racial groups

---

20. Buell, *Why This New Race*, xiii.

limiting and perhaps odd. This is not to say that skin color was not noticed or a discerning factor. They certainly did notice physical differences between people groups and linked these aspects to racial identity. But there was no such thing as a "white," "black," or "brown" identity. Instead, they turned to environmental, genealogical, and cultural factors to help explain physical and character differences among people groups.

Environmental Factors

The Romans recognized the environment's impact among racial groups. For example, the Scythians were known to have light skin because they lived in the extreme northern region of the known world.[21] Likewise, Ethiopians, who lived in the most southern part of the Roman Empire, were known to have dark skin.[22] When we observe more closely how the Greeks and Romans explained these features, the environment did more than simply influence the physical development and appearance of racial groups. It was believed that the environment also impacted the character and intellect of its inhabitants. Balsdon finds that the Romans took this environmental racial theory to help explain their military success. The Romans believed that those who lived near the equator such as the Ethiopians were considered small and to suffer from blood deficiencies that made them bad fighters.[23] Northerners, on the other hand, were tall, deep-voiced, pale-faced, and full-blooded fighters who were courageous but foolish in battle. Since the Romans lived in neither the extreme north or south, this naturally made the Rome superior to the northerners in terms of intelligence and superior to the southerners in terms of physical strength.[24] In other words, environmental determinism was a racial ideology used to

---

21. Ptolemy, *Tetra*. 2.2.
22. Pliny, *Nat*. 2.80.
23. Balsdon, *Romans and Aliens*, 59.
24. Balsdon, *Romans and Aliens*, 60.

explain not only differences among people groups but also why the Roman Empire was victorious.

This, however, is not simply a Roman idea. It was a deeply pervasive racial ideology that can be traced back to the early Greeks, who also made comments and observations about the various people who lived throughout the known Mediterranean world. The origins of environmental determinism can be traced to Hippocrates's *On Airs, Waters, Places*. Hippocrates asserts that each region has its own weather with distinct soil and inhabitants. In comparison to both these extremes, those who live in moderate temperatures are considered healthier. He states:

> Those that lie toward the risings of the sun are likely to be healthier than those facing the north and those exposed to the hot winds. . . . In the first place, the heat and the cold are more moderate. . . . For the sun, shining down upon them when it rises, purifies them. The persons of the inhabitants are of better complexion and more blooming than elsewhere, unless some disease prevents this. They are clear-voiced, and with better temper and intelligence than those who are exposed to the north, just as all things growing there are better.[25]

Notice in the above quote how Hippocrates believes that the weather has a major impact on the aesthetic, health, moral, and intellectual aspect of human identity. One cannot avoid being sicker and aesthetically unpleasing if one resides in either a northern or southern area. Hippocrates finds a strong correlation between one's environment and character, which also includes the reason why Europeans are not ruled by kings but have a rugged individualistic, intelligent, brave, and warlike temperament.[26]

This view, also known as environmental determinism, was later developed by Greek writers such as Plato, Aristotle, and Polybius.[27] They, too, explained the relationship between the environment and the character and physical appearances of various racial

---

25. Hippocrates, *Airs, Waters, Places* 5.10–5.28.
26. Hippocrates, *Airs, Waters, Places* 24.1–25.67.
27. Plato, *Leg.* 747d–e; Aristotle, *Physiogn.* 806b15; Polybius, *Hist.* 4.21.

groups. By the time the Romans emerged on the scene, this view was politically useful to justify the conquest and superiority of the Roman race. Vitruvius, a Roman writer, thus asserts:

> The races of Italy are the most perfectly constituted in both respects—in bodily form and in mental activity to correspond to their valor. Exactly as the planet Jupiter is itself temperate, its course lying midway between Mars, which is very hot, and so Italy, lying between the north and the south, is a combination of what is found on each side, and Saturn, which is very cold, so Italy, lying between the north and the south, is a combination of what is found on each side, and her preeminence is well regulated and indisputable. (*Arch.* 6.1.11)

While this racial theory also contributed to Roman imperial propaganda, it is also important to note that not everyone embraced this belief. Furthermore, this view is also relative to where one considers the "center" of the world. In Jewish literature, Jerusalem is the center of the world, and all other nations are geographically spaced in relation to it.[28] This racial ideology reflected more about how one geographically arranged the environment of racial groups in relation to oneself.

While we do not find many statements that reflect the racial ideology of environmental determinism, some comments do emerge. There are hints in the New Testament that one's identity was reflective of the origin of one's region. Paul quotes a common stereotypical view of the Cretans as "liars," "evil beasts," and "lazy gluttons" (Titus 1:12). The Galatians are described as "foolish," reflective of common intellectual assessments of people who live in distant lands (Gal 3:1). Nathanael doubts whether anything good could come from Nazareth when he realizes this is Jesus's hometown (John 1:46). Some view the disciples with suspicion for speaking and coming from Galilee (Matt 26:69–73; Acts 2:7–8). And Judea is portrayed throughout Roman literature as the eastern part of the empire, where corrupting influences originate.[29]

---

28. Isa 60:1–16; Jub. 8:19; Ezek 38:12; b. Sanh. 37a.
29. Florus, *Epit. rom. hist.* 1.47.12.7–1.47.12.8.

Overall, the boundaries of the known Roman world were not viewed with much suspicion by the earliest Christian evangelist. For example, while the Scythians and Ethiopians were viewed as those who lived in the extreme limits of the Roman world, they were also mentioned as people who should hear the gospel. Paul makes mention of his desire to preach the gospel to the Scythians (Col 3:11). Luke describes the conversion of an Ethiopian eunuch by Philip (Acts 8:30–39). Likewise, the gospel given to the disciples was not for their own native region alone; it was to be proclaimed to "the remotest parts of the earth" (Acts 1:8). The universal mission of the gospel stems from Jesus's commission to the disciples and his first followers.[30]

While the environment at first helped explain phenotypes between people groups, what is most harmful is the assumption made between the environment and the intellectual and moral capabilities of such individuals or racial groups. Overall, this view is fundamentally contrary to the message of the gospel, which teaches the human worth, dignity, and salvation of all people. What makes this racial belief ultimately irreconcilable with the Christian faith is that the moral, intellectual potential, and value of human beings are linked to the climate and land in which racial groups reside. Geography, in other words, is utilized to justify inhuman treatment of people.

Genealogical Factors

Ancients also utilized the criterion of genealogy to understand racial differences. This by far was one of the most important and fundamental aspects of defining the boundaries between racial groups. Jonathan Hall finds that the ancient Greeks used genealogies to anchor an individual to a group of ancestors of a particular racial group.[31] This does not mean that the genealogies were accurate. This really did not matter for the ancients. What mattered

---

30. Matt 28:19; Mark 16:15–20; Luke 24:47; John 20:20.
31. J. Hall, *Ethnic Identity*, 25–28.

was that the claim for a shared descent was consensually agreed.³² Caroline Hodge likewise explores the importance of genealogical relations when traced through a male line and his descendants. Also known as "patrilineal ideology," Hodge explains that this ideology socially organized families through a common ancestor, included the assumption that descendants inherit the ancestor's characteristics, and understood that the corporate group was organically linked together.³³

Genealogies were indeed utilized to invoke a particular identity that one inherited from an apical ancestor. For example, Alexander the Great was considered a descendant of Hercules, which, as Diodorus remarks, gave him the "inherited physical and moral qualities of greatness."³⁴ This common conviction continues within Jewish literature. Josephus, in fact, begins his life story by first pointing out his noble lineage and ancestors. He states, "My family is no ignoble one, tracing its descent far back to priestly ancestors."³⁵ Josephus also explains that while different races may base their claims to nobility on various options, for the Jewish people the connection to the priesthood was "the hallmark of an illustrious line."³⁶ There was also the recognition that King Herod, an Edomite, tried to rewrite his genealogy by commissioning Nicholas of Damascus to link his identity to a Jewish lineage descending from Babylon.³⁷ While this may appear humorous, it testifies to the need of a king to claim a more noble lineage over the Jewish people he rules.

The opening of Matthew's Gospel states the following, "This is the genealogy of Jesus the Messiah the son of David, the son of Abraham" (Matt 1:1). We might have read these verses and skipped over them. Honestly, genealogies are perhaps not the most inspiring thing to read. In the ancient world, though, one of the

32. J. Hall, *Ethnic Identity*, 25.
33. Hodge, *If Sons, Then Heirs*, 22–23.
34. Diodorus, *Bib. hist.* 17.1.5; 17.4.1.
35. Josephus, *Life* 1.1.
36. Josephus, *Life* 1.1–2.
37. Josephus, *Jewish Antiquities* 14.9.

Ancient Racial Ideologies

most popular ways of understanding racial difference and belonging was in terms of lineages. Reading the lineage not only identifies Jesus's racial identity, but it also places Jesus within a kingly lineage as a descendant of King David. Last, Paul himself also boasts of his lineage as well, as a "Pharisee descended from Pharisees" (Acts 23:6) and "of the people of Israel, of the tribe of Benjamin, a Hebrew of Hebrews" (Phil 3:5). He reminds people of his heritage and in a sense uses a genealogical argument to assert the honor, prestige, and status he inherited from his ancestors.

Tell me who your ancestors are, and I can know and understand your identity. This would have been the racial logic in the ancient world. Lineage was everything in the ancient world. It justified power and prestige, including the right to rule. Although useful in determining family relations and maintaining a cohesive group identity by appealing to shared ancestors, it also had limitations. This racial ideology certainly had the potential to justify segregationist attitudes, especially if it was believed that the quality of an entire people was determined by lineage preservation. In fact, Isaac recognizes that for some, genealogical purity signified racial superiority.[38] This racial ideology, as a result, would put immigrants and foreigners in a status of perpetual suspicion. It also could be used to rationalize the inhumane treatment of racial groups on the assumption that racial mixture among different groups would produce inferior descendants.

However, this racial ideology was important for the emergence of early Christian self-understanding. Within the New Testament, we also find how the gentile mission and inclusion was explained in terms of a lineage racial logic. We see this specifically in Paul's dialogue on the role of Abraham and the role faith has in incorporating gentiles into the family of God (Gal 3:6–9). For Paul, the promise God gave to Abraham's descendants is not only to those related to him through genealogical relations, but it also includes those related to Abraham through faith in God (Rom 4:12–16). Who were those incorporated in the line of Abraham? Gentiles! In fact, Hodge remarks that Paul "constructs for them

---

38. Isaac, *Invention of Racism*, 109–48.

a myth of origins which is intimately tied to Jewish origins."[39] Indeed, Gal 3:27, most often quoted to explain why race does not matter, is actually a racial argument. Paul explains that since believers have faith in Jesus, they have become children of God and belong to Christ. As a result of this new linkage to Christ and God through faith, they are thus incorporated into the lineage of Abraham (Gal 3:26–29). The theology of Paul in these passages makes sense only when we understand that Paul is using a racial argument to explain how gentiles have been incorporated into the family of God and thus receive the promises God gave to Abraham and his descendants.

This is not to suggest that this racial argument was the most important factor. Sometimes, lineages were subverted. This is most specifically noticed in the Gospel of John when it asserts that the children of God are those defined not in terms of their ancestry but due to being born into the lineage of God (John 1:11–13).[40] When reading the biblical text, we must stay mindful of the ways the racial logic of genealogies is used to construct or deconstruct racial identity.

Nonetheless, being a descendant of an important figure was no small matter. Identifying one's racial identity according to one's lineage also invoked the honor and privileges that come from an apical ancestor. Buell indeed notes that Christians used genealogical myths of descent to define themselves with a respected pedigree by asserting historical relation to key figures such as Abraham and Jesus.[41] This should disabuse us of the notion that race did not matter in the ancient world. It proved vital not only for understanding the identity of Jesus and Paul, but also to help explain how believers can now incorporate into the family of God.

---

39. Hodge, *If Sons, Then Heirs*, 85.
40. Estrada, *Latino Reading of Race*, 111–34.
41. Buell, *Why This New Race*, 75–76, 90–91.

Cultural Factors

Apart from lineage and environment, culture was an important manner for understanding oneself and others. Culture was a distinguishing mark of racial groups. Indeed, the Romans were known to value morality and culture more than lineage.[42] The Roman elite even assumed that the goal of Roman imperialism was to civilize humanity with Roman culture.[43] While culture separated various racial groups, sometimes culture also provided proof of a common racial identity. During the emergence of the Roman Empire, some writers desired to trace the beginnings of the Latin people. Virgil's *Aeneid* is one popular attempt to link the Romans as descendants of Aeneas, a Trojan who escaped and migrated to Italy after the war and fall of Troy. Dionysius of Halicarnassus, a Greek historian during the reign of Augustus, also attempts to prove that the Romans are truly descendants of the Greek Trojans by appealing to their common customs,[44] insisting,

> In these cities there survived for a very long time many of the ancient customs formerly in use among the Greeks, such as the fashion of their arms of war . . . and whenever they sent out an army beyond their borders, either to begin a war or to resist an invasion, certain holy men, unarmed, went ahead of the rest bearing the terms of peace; similar, also, were the structure of their temples, the images of their gods, their purifications and sacrifices and many other things of that nature.[45]

Like Virgil, Dionysius links the Romans to the Greeks by appealing to their common lineage. But Dionysius adds further proof of this connection. He points to their similar cultural traditions, which includes their weapons of war, religion, and sacrifices. More specifically, he points out that it was the "temple of Juno" that the Romans built in the same style of the one that was built

42. Woolf, "Becoming Roman," 130.
43. Pliny, *Nat.* 3.6.
44. Dionysius of Halicarnassus, *Roman Antiquities* 1.5.2; 1.89.1–1.89.2.
45 Dionysius of Halicarnassus, *Roman Antiquities* 1.21.1.

in Argos, a Greek city (*Ant. rom.* 1.21.2). Common cultural practices with the Trojan Greeks, in other words, served as proof of Roman racial identity.

Shared cultural traditions were utilized not only to prove the Roman identity but also to define the Greek identity. Isocrates claimed that being a Greek was not simply a lineage claim but an "intelligence" and that the name Greek could be applied to those who shared the Greek culture.[46] Alexander the Great also attempted to redefine the Greek identity as he expanded and influenced various regions with Greek culture. For Alexander, a Greek was defined in terms of virtue, and barbarians were defined in terms of their iniquity.[47] This redefinition of the Greek identity in terms of morality was not only a move away from an emphasis on lineage and environment but also opened the possibility for recently conquered subjects to become Greek. Specifically, Greekness began to be viewed as a cultural way of life; it did not simply mean having a particular association with an apical ancestor or territory. Anyone could become Greek if they decided to live like a Greek and be formed in the Greek way of life.

Cultural traditions became definitive proof of racial identity during the Roman age. It was not simply lineage or appeal to a common homeland that defined one's racial identity. McCoskey, in fact, points out that racial identity was both "formed and performed."[48] This helps us recognize not only the malleability of racial identity but also the need to maintain racial identity through one's way of life.[49] Furthermore, Jonathan Hall adds that cultural performance as a marker of racial identity seems to have been more important over time.[50] That is, one can become associated, classified, or belong to a racial group based on daily activities, habits, and lifestyle practices. Being a Greek or Roman meant living like a Greek or Roman. This also suggests that racial identity was

---

46. Isocrates, *Paneg.* 50.
47. Plutarch, *Alexander* 329.c–d.
48. McCoskey, *Race*, 81.
49. Estrada, "Racial Significance of Paul's Clothing."
50. J. Hall, *Hellenicity*, 189–220.

not permanent. One could possibly be influenced by the cultures of other racial groups and thus lose or develop a racial identity.

While culture was distinguishable between people groups, what mattered most was the way in which culture structured and organized one's way of life according to the customs and habits accepted and approved by the racial group. Yet culture as a way of life also becomes an easy target to disparage, especially when compared to the "civilized" Romans or Greeks. In several instances within Greek and Roman literature, the superiority or inferiority of racial groups was judged on their closeness to Roman and Greek culture. People were considered "barbarian" simply for being non-Greek. Indeed, Edith Hall remarks that the idea of a "barbarian" was created to serve as a "universal anti-Greek against whom Hellenic—especially Athenian—culture was defined."[51] Some, however, objected to the assertion of essential differences between Greeks and barbarians. Cicero, a Roman statesman writing in 51 BCE during the Republic of Rome, narrates a debate between Scipio and Laelius on whether Romulus, the founder of Rome, was a king of barbarians. Laelius states, "If that name [barbarian] ought to be applied on the basis of men's manners rather than their language, I do not consider the Greeks less barbarous than the Romans." Scipio also responds by suggesting that "character, not race" ought to define one as a barbarian.[52] In this short dialogue, character and customs define the barbarian, not association or non-association to the Greek identity.

While culture served as an important factor for understanding racial identity in the Greek and Roman world, it was also a limited marker of racial identity, given that every act or material object may not have equal significance.[53] This suggests that the cultural practices themselves must be a meaningful marker of one's identity and used to either define one's group or serve to contrast to another racial group.

51. E. Hall, *Inventing the Barbarian*, 5.
52. Cicero, *On the Republic* 1.58.
53. McCoskey, *Race*, 86.

RACE IS EVERYWHERE

Studying race in the ancient world requires that we understand how the ancients understood this concept in their own terms, not with respect to our modern categories. Once we do so, it should help disabuse us of the notion that race did not exist in the ancient world and that they found the concept unimportant. In the Mediterranean world, the notion of race and ethnicity emerged most clearly when people groups were defined, classified, or differentiated. "Race" and "ethnicity" are terms used to understand the boundaries between people groups.

As we have observed, environmental conditions not only helped explain physical differences between racial groups, but it was also believed that the environment impacted the innate character of people groups. The Greeks and Romans used environmental determinism to justify conquest and imperial domination of foreigners. While this view ultimately was a way to stereotypically describe the intellectual and character traits of racial groups, it fundamentally stands contrary to the gospel belief in the human dignity of all people. The ancients tied racial identity to environment. "Tell me which region you are from, and I can know who you are" would have been a common way of understanding people groups.

Regarding genealogies, the ancients understood the importance of their ancestors and relation to others by means of them. Genealogies were open, negotiable, and vital for the understanding of one's identity, especially if one was related to a heroic ancestor or god. Genealogies helped people understand kinship relations, assisted in political diplomacy, were utilized to invoke moral or character traits, and in some cases, became a tool to justify the segregation between racial groups. People in the ancient world would have asked, "Tell me who your ancestors were, and I will know who you are." Racial identity was derived from a linkage to one's ancestors.

Culture, likewise, was an important factor in defining racial groups. It was not about how one looked, who one's ancestor was, or where one was born. One could say, "Tell me how you live, and

I will know who you are." It was about how one lived that enabled one to become classified or to join a racial group. While some were open to the customs and practices of racial groups, others found cultural influences a threat. This also suggests that racial identity was fluid and liable to change. What mattered most, though, was whether the cultural marker had racial significance for the racial group.

Perhaps now, at the minimum, we are more attuned to those aspects in Scripture that we casually glanced over or did not even notice. Hopefully you can now see "race" all around you, especially as it emerges within the Gospel of John. Racial identity was very important for the ancients, and for early Christians specifically as they emerged and defined their own identity in light of contesting ones. For them, one's homeland, genealogies, and culture were matters of race, and this, too, was vital for their own self-understanding.

3

Marking One's Birth by the Spirit (John 3)

THE DIALOGUE BETWEEN JESUS and Nicodemus has posed a literary riddle for many interpreters.[1] Nicodemus meets Jesus in the night and greets him by saying, "Rabbi, we know that you have come from God, teacher, for no one is able to do these miracles which you do, unless God is with you" (John 3:2). Jesus responds to Nicodemus's greeting with an immediate discussion about being born again. Jesus states, "Amen, amen, I say to you, unless one is born again, one is not able to see the kingdom of God" (v. 3). Why such a response to Nicodemus's greeting? What was of such grave importance that Jesus preferred to discuss with a "ruler of the Jews" (3:1) the role of the Spirit as an entrance requirement into the kingdom of God? Perhaps Jesus was alerted to this topic because Nicodemus greeted him with the assertion that Jesus is

---

1. Raymond Brown, Charles H. Dodd, and Barnabas Lindars each notice that the dialogue turns into a monologue from vv. 11–21 (R. Brown, *Gospel According to John*, 1:144–45; Dodd, *Interpretation of Fourth Gospel*, 303; Lindars, *Gospel of John*, 146); George Beasley-Murray contends that it is doubtful that the evangelist intended the readers to hear vv. 13–21 and vv. 31–36 as the voice of Christ (*John*, 46); Leon Morris admits that the writer seems to speak through the story, but it is difficult to know where it begins (*John*, 202).

from God,² or maybe Jesus already seemed to know what was on Nicodemus's mind and began the conversation without allowing him to ask a question.³

Nonetheless, the conversation between Nicodemus and Jesus centers around the need to be "born again" as a requirement to see the kingdom of God.⁴ In their conversation, Jesus also uses the phrase "born of water and Spirit" (John 3:5) and compares those "born of the Spirit" with those of the flesh and the natural wind (vv. 6, 8). In fact, there is so much birth talk that Nicodemus misunderstands Jesus's statement and asserts the impossibility of being physically born for the second time (v. 4). Though Jesus commences a lengthy monologue after this brief conversation, Nicodemus gradually disappears from the story. We do not know what ever happened to Nicodemus after he met with Jesus that night. Did Nicodemus come to faith? Did he slip back into his home before anyone saw him? Though Nicodemus's whereabouts that night are unknown, he emerges much later in the Gospel story (7:50–53) and becomes an important figure who, along with Joseph of Arimathea, buries the body of Jesus (19:39–42).

With such a focus on this birthing language, what does it mean to be "born" of the Spirit? This last question is the focus of this chapter. In fact, various scholars have attempted to answer this question by proposing that this language refers to the sacraments⁵

---

2. R. Brown, *Gospel According to John*, 1:138; William Grese suggests that this affirmation that Jesus has come from God is a request for more revelation ("Unless One Is Born Again"); Tricia Brown finds Nicodemus's greeting as one that includes an inadequate estimation of Jesus's identity, which triggered a response (*Spirit in Writings of John*, 118).

3. Lindars, *Gospel of John*, 150.

4. We often feel unsure whether Jesus's focus was on being born from "above" or being born "again," given that the Greek word ἄνωθεν can be translated as "from above" (John 19:11; Jas 1:17; 3:15, 17), "from the beginning" (Luke 1:3; John 19:23; Acts 26:5), or "from the top" (Matt 27:51; Mark 15:38). In this translation, "again" is preferred, given that this is what prompted Nicodemus's reaction and the ensuing clarification (also Gal 4:9). Regardless, this should not distract us from the main concern about the necessity of a new "birth," which appears eight times in this dialogue.

5. Barrett, *St. John*, 174; Beasley-Murray, *John*, 55; Dodd, *Interpretation of*

or an understanding of salvation in terms of spiritual rebirth.[6] While these views are not mutually exclusive, what has not been explored is how the discussion about being "born again" really involves a discussion about lineage and relation with one's ancestors.

What do I mean by this? As explored in the previous chapter, to talk about one's birth is also the way people in the ancient world discussed racial identity and race relations. They mentioned their birth relations to their ancestors whenever they desired to show affiliation or membership to a particular racial group. What we find here, in John 3:1–10, is an argument for the racial inclusion of non-Jewish people within the family of God. When we step back and think about John's community, the readers of the Gospel, it would have been these non-Jews who were mostly concerned about their place within the family of God because they did not have a Jewish lineage or heritage. This dialogue, though, is not just about the inclusion of non-Jews into the family of God—it is about all people. And given that Jesus has this dialogue with Nicodemus, perhaps some Jewish leaders like Nicodemus also felt hesitant about the inclusion of non-Jewish members as well. This is not to suppose that all were resistant. However, it makes sense if this teaching was triggered by some Greeks, Romans, or Samaritans within John's community who started to make claims that they were going to reign with God but did not have any lineage ties to the promises of the Jewish patriarchs—especially Abraham.

To support this reading, we will first reread the birthing language and how claims of genealogical descent are challenged with an appeal to the Spirit. The conversation between Jesus and Nicodemus not only articulates the Spirit's participation in the incorporation of both Jews and non-Jews; it also reflects a question that the Johannine community had about those being admitted to faith in Jesus. Together, this reading will help us not only

---

Fourth Gospel, 308; Lindars, *Gospel of John*, 152; Burge, *Anointed Community*, 150–58.

6. Barrett, *St. John*, 170–74; R. Brown, *Gospel According to John*, 1:144–45; Beasley-Murray, *John*, 55; Belleville, "Born of Water and Spirit," 140; Grese, "Unless One is Born Again."

understand the meaning of this conversation but also see how the Spirit's involvement in rebirth served as an argument that justified the inclusion of diverse racial groups within the family of God—that is, God's kingdom.

CONTEMPORARY VIEWS ON "BORN" AGAIN

The term "born" is the Greek word γεννάω, which can be translated as "begetting," "bearing," or simply to be "born." It describes a child begotten of a father, women who bear children, or figuratively explains things brought forth, produced, or caused.[7] We find the notion of being "begotten" akin to the idea of a divine begetting.[8] Even more, this language is also utilized within rabbinic literature to describe converts who have been born like a child.[9] As a result, thinking about race may not naturally come to mind when we come across this passage that discusses the need to be born of the Spirit. Indeed, this is such a popular passage in contemporary Christianity that we may define ourselves as "born-again" believers. The language John's Gospel uses, though, is one used in terms of linking people according to their ancestral lineage.

When we explore the noting of being born throughout the Gospel, various references describe both human and divine begetting. As we can notice from the below chart, most of the birthing language refers to human birth. Most references to divine birth are mentioned in the Prologue (John 1:1–18) and Jesus's dialogue with Nicodemus (3:1–10).

Below are the following uses in John's Gospel:

---

7. "γεννάω," BDAG 55b–d; Friedrich Büchsel, "γεννάω," *TDNT* 1:662–65.
8. Menken, "Born of God," 366.
9. b. Yeb. 22a; 62a; 97b; b. Ber. 47a.

Divine Birth		Human Birth	
1:13	were born of God	3:4	a person born
3:3	born again	3:4	born from womb of mother
3:5	born of water and Spirit	3:6	born of flesh
3:6	born of Spirit	8:41	born of fornication
3:7	born again	9:2	born blind
3:8	born of Spirit	9:19	born blind
		9:20	born blind
		9:32	having been born blind
		9:34	born in sin
		16:21	births a child
		16:21	a child born
		18:37	in this I have been born

This birthing imagery has challenged scholars and has raised questions on whether this language denotes a feminine aspect in God.[10] Sandra Schneiders finds that these passages are perhaps the clearest passage in the New Testament where female imagery occurs, similar to the parental metaphors in Deut 32:18 where God gives birth to Israel.[11] Annette Weissenrieder also argues that John 1:12–13 and 3:3–8 refer to ancient family imagery applied to believers. She insists that the reader must wait until the resurrection before the disciples experience this link to God as children.[12] Others, such as Adele Reinhartz, read this birthing language in terms of ancient medical embryology.[13] Reinhartz argues that Jesus's begottenness resembles the human procreation process, which

10. Menken, "Born of God," 366; Schneiders, "Born Anew," 194; Weissenrieder, "Spirit and Rebirth," 77.

11. Schneiders, "Born Anew," 194. See also Ps 2:7; Prov 8:25; Hos 5:7; Isa 1:2; 66:9. Philo also describes God as the begetter of all things, including humanity (*Leg.* 3.219; *Conf.* 1.63; *Mut.* 1.29). Paul utilizes this birthing imagery when describing communities and individuals in 1 Cor 4:15; Gal 4:19; Philm 1:10.

12. Weissenrieder, "Spirit and Rebirth," 79.

13. Reinhartz, "Word Was Begotten." See Aristotle, *Gen. an.* 716a1–15; 731b25; 735b10; 766b15–769a22.

was influenced by Aristotle's theory of epigenesis.¹⁴ According to Aristotle, as Reinhartz notes, seminal fluid was understood as both "water and spirit."¹⁵ As such, Reinhartz affirms that a child of God is one begotten of the divine seed that originates in the upper cosmos.¹⁶ While this reading resonates with the natural birthing functions and procreation, others suggest that this birthing language, especially since it includes the notion of being born of "water and spirit" (v. 5), reflects a sacramental view of baptism or ritual cleansing.¹⁷ Still others suggest that this language refers simply to the power of God beyond human comprehension or ability.¹⁸

The views above all agree that the notion of being born by the Spirit is a divine act beyond human control. They differ on the significance of the birthing language, whether it refers to birth through a divine seed, refers to baptism, echoes a ritual cleansing imagery, or reflects God's divine power. Raymond Brown, however, suggests that this dialogue is not about the need to have a Christian baptism or ritual cleansing, though it can be interpreted as such.¹⁹ Instead, he suggests that John is attempting to explain how believers are considered sons of God, similar to how Paul utilized adoption language.²⁰ Why use this birthing metaphor,

---

14. Reinhartz, "Word Was Begotten," 86.

15. Reinhartz, "Word Was Begotten," 89–92. Aristotle believed seminal fluid was composed of water and *pneuma* (*Gen. an.* 735b–736a); Ben Witherington likewise argues against a sacramental reading of "water" and argues that this is a "terminus technicus" for matters involving procreation, childbearing capacity, or the act of giving birth itself ("Waters of Birth").

16. Reinhartz, "Word Was Begotten," 96; 1 Pet 1:23 and 1 John 3:9 also utilize this metaphor.

17. Morris, *Gospel According to John*, 192–93; Burge, *Anointed Community*, 162–63, 169, 170–75; Dodd, *Interpretation of Fourth Gospel*, 309–10; Lindars, *Gospel of John*, 148–52; Barrett, *St. John*, 174–76; Grese, "Unless One Is Born Again," 680–84. See also Ps 51:7; Isa 4:4; Jer 33:8; Ezek 36:25–26; Jub. 1:23–25; Philo, *Mos.* 2.138–39.

18. Bultmann, *Gospel of John*, 139n1; Morris, *Gospel According to John*, 188; Johnston, *Spirit-Paraclete*, 10.

19. R. Brown, *Gospel According to John*, 1:142.

20. R. Brown, *Gospel According to John*, 1:140–45. See also Gal 4:5; Rom 8:23; Titus 3:5.

however, in a dialogue with Nicodemus? Asked differently, what concrete reality lies at the base of this abstract language?

BORN OF THE SPIRIT AS RACIAL LANGUAGE

Today, we often do not think about our identities in a collectivist manner, but in the ancient Greek and Roman worlds, lineages were everything. People who are born are born into racial groups—tribes, clans, and most importantly, families. They are placed in relation not only to their immediate family but also their historic ancestors, who shape their identity. Jonathan Hall points out that the myth of a common descent is one of the most distinguishing characteristics of a racial group, especially since social groups do not presume to share genealogical relations.[21] Even though some genealogical relations are fabricated or exaggerated, there is still an assumption that a person can justify their right to be included within the racial group by the nature of birth. Scholars traditionally emphasize the theological implications of John's birthing language and the possible baptism allusion to the phrase "water and Spirit" (v. 5). However, the Greek word γεννάω is the same word utilized when a newly born child is linked to an ancestor.

The concern to trace one's lineage also appears with Hebrew patriarchs, Israelite kings, and in the Gospels' record of Jesus's lineage. The term γεννάω appears frequently to describe sons begotten by their fathers, a lineage network traced to an apical male ancestor.[22] We see this not only in the Old Testament when Adam's lineage is recounted but also with Jesus's lineage that connects him with Abraham. Lineages in both the Old and New Testaments have a vital function in communicating the identity of individuals and groups.[23] Again, we cannot fail to recognize that being born

---

21. J. Hall, *Ethnic Identity*, 25.

22. Gen 5:3–32; 10:8—11:27; 25:19; 46:20–21; Ruth 4:18–22; 1 Chr 1:1—9:44; Matt 1:2–16. Luke, however, avoids using γεννάω and explains Jesus's ancestry in terms of sonship (3:23–38).

23. K. C. Hanson asserts that genealogies establish a significant kinship group to which one belongs (2 Sam 9:6), embody the honor of the family in a

Marking One's Birth by the Spirit (John 3)

means more than simply expanding the nuclear family. It signifies the entrance into a family that is linked to a history of ancestors, relatives, and a larger racial community.

We see this aspect throughout Greek literature, which uses the same birthing language (γεννάω) to describe one's relationship and responsibility to the wider city and community. Take, for example, Plato's *Crito*, when Socrates debates how one should respond to the unjust verdict of a judge. Socrates concludes that one is still obligated to receive the judgment regardless of the outcome. He is confident with this reasoning because he recognizes that the individual is indebted to the Greek city on the grounds of birth. He assumes that if one would reject the verdict of the judge, the Greek city would say,

> Come on then, what blame do you attach to us and the city, that you are attempting to destroy us? Wasn't it we who gave you birth [ἐγεννήσαμεν] in the first place, and your father married your mother through us and gave you life?[24]

Here we find that it was the collective city, as well as a father and mother, who birthed Socrates. Later we also find this similar birthing language to describe Socrates's relationship with the wider Greek community. Socrates presumes that the Athenians will claim that they birthed, educated, nurtured, and gave him a share of all the good things from the city.[25]

Yet the Athenian Greeks did not only express their racial identity with birthing language, but they also held the notion that their original ancestors were born from the land and thus

---

list of names (1 Sam 9:1), identify potential marriage partners (Josephus, *Jewish Antiquities* 17.12–17.16), identify outsiders (Josephus, *Jewish Antiquities* 18.130–18.141), make a political claim to leadership (1 Kgs 13:2), assert an inheritance or family rights (2 Sam 3:2–5; 5:13–16), establish membership in the religious group (1 Chr 9:1; Ezra 2:59–63; 10:18–44), and establish the right to hereditary offices (Exod 28:1; Lev 16:32) ("All in the Family," 30–31).

24. Plato, *Crito* 50d.
25. Plato, *Crito* 51c.

originated from the earth.²⁶ Again, Socrates explains the land's relation to their Athenian ancestors through birthing language:

> The whole earth was putting forth and producing animals of every kind, wild and tame, our country showed herself barren and void of wild animals but chose for herself and gave birth [ἐγέννησεν] to man, who surpasses all other animals in intelligence and alone of animals regards justice and the gods. And we have a signal proof of this statement in that this land of ours has given birth to the forefathers both of these men and of ourselves . . . for it is not the country that imitates the woman in the matter of conception and birth [γεννησαμένη], but the woman the country.²⁷

We thus notice that this birthing language was much more connected to one's land, city, and community, not just the immediate family. In fact, the Athenians claim to be people born from the land, a notion that draws upon the biological act of giving birth. For these ancient Athenians, a woman's natural ability to give birth mirrors the earth's ability to give birth to humanity. Since the land gave birth to their ancestors, the descendants are responsible for keeping civic polity and the traditions of the gods.²⁸

Knowing one's ancestors was vital to one's place and relation to others. Lineages were also utilized to mitigate conflicts,

---

26. Plato remarks, "But then, Stranger, how did animals come into existence in those days? How were they begotten [ἐγεννῶντο] of one another? It is clear, Socrates, that being begotten [γεννώμενον] of one another was no part of the natural order of that time, but the earth-born [γηγενὲς] race which, according to tradition, once existed, was the race which returned at that time out of the earth; and the memory of it was preserved by our earliest ancestors . . . for this reason they are inevitably earth-born [γηγενεῖς], and hence arises their name and the tradition about them, except those of them whom God removed to some other fate" (*Statesman* 271a-c).

27. Plato, *Menexenus* 237d–238a.

28. Socrates continues: "We and our people, on the contrary, being all born of one mother, claim to be neither the slaves of one another nor the masters; rather does our natural birth-equality drive us to seek lawfully legal equality, and to yield to one another in no respect save in reputation for virtue and understanding" (*Menexenus* 2389a).

support political allies, and create a more reputable origin story.[29] Lineages enabled the ancients to define the boundaries of their racial groups while explaining an individual's relationship to his or her community and land. For some, such as the Athenians and Spartans, this not only led them to suspect foreigners, but it also helped ensure that members within the community had clear boundaries and duties. We also find a similar logic when heroes or rulers drew upon their ancestry to explain their power or heroic deeds. We thus find the Homeric hero Odysseus described as the Zeus-sired son of Laertes,[30] Alexander the Great as the son of god Zeus-Ammon,[31] and the Roman Emperor Caesar Augustus was regarded as the son of the god Apollo.[32] Philo also proposes different types of people, those who are "earth-born," "heaven-born," and "God-born."[33] He insists that priests and prophets are "men of God" (θεοῦ δὲ ἄνθρωποι), different than the cosmopolitans of the world.[34] Early Christians also caught on to the importance of being associated to a honorable ancestor. Denise Buell finds that myths of descent were regularly utilized by Christians to define themselves with a respected pedigree by inserting themselves in relation to key figures such as Abraham and Jesus.[35]

Overall, this concern with "birth" in the ancient world also means that we need to have the wider network of ancestors in mind. This understanding of lineages and the significance of one's birth now presents us with some problems when we turn to the emergence of early Christianity. While gentiles were known to convert to Judaism, this did not mean that gentiles automatically shared a genealogical relation to Jewish ancestors. Scot McKnight

---

29. Herodotus, *Hist.* 7.150; Thucydides, *Hist.* 6.2.1–6.6.3; Dionysius of Halicarnassus, *Roman Antiquities* 1.89–90.

30. Homer, *Iliad* 10.144.

31. Plutarch, *Alexander* 2.1—3.2.

32. Suetonius, *Aug.* 94.4.

33. Philo, *On the Giants* 60.

34. Philo, *On the Giants* 61.

35. Buell, *Why This New Race*, 75–76; Buell and Hodge, "Politics of Interpretation."

finds hints at this issue with the status of gentile converts; he notes that despite a positive reception, converted gentiles might have never been seen as fully Jewish, including female proselytes.[36] They might have been officially recognized and socially integrated but always remained as gentiles.[37] In other words, the convert, although equally loved and welcomed, was always seen as a convert, not on the same status of other Jews who shared a direct lineage to Abraham.

Shaye Cohen argues this point when he traces the conversion ceremony and status of gentiles in rabbinic literature. He points to m. Bik. 1.4–5, which states,

> The convert brings but does not recite, because he cannot say (the land) which God has sworn to our fathers to give us. But if his mother was of Israel, he brings and recites. And when he prays by himself, he says, "God of the fathers of Israel." And when he is in the synagogue he says, "God of your fathers."

As the above quote notes, only Jews who have a direct lineage to the patriarchs can confidently describe God as the father of Israel. Cohen regards this text as evidence that the convert suffers a legal disability because of his or her non-Jewish lineage.[38] He notices that converts constitute a separate lineage or caste within Jewish society because they lack a Jewish father.[39] The Mishnah, in this sense, reflects the value of a Jewish pedigree and purity of genealogical descent. As a result, converts will never be fully equal with the native Jews because they lack a genuine Jewish lineage that incorporates them into the family of the patriarchs—Abraham, Isaac, and Jacob.[40]

Now, John's Gospel is not the only writer concerned about the inclusion of gentiles or the only one who challenged the exclusion

---

36. McKnight, *Light Among the Gentiles*, 38–45.
37. McKnight, *Light Among the Gentiles*, 101.
38. Cohen, *Beginnings of Jewishness*, 309.
39. Cohen, *Beginnings of Jewishness*, 324.
40. Cohen, *Beginnings of Jewishness*, 325.

that lineages create. It was possible for gentiles to convert to Judaism and even join a Jewish community. Philo recognized the risk that converts take, given that they are "abandoning their kinsfolk by blood, their country, their customs and the temples and images of their gods."[41] It was a major risk for gentiles to join a new community. As such, Philo remarks that the Jewish people were taught by Moses to "love the incomers, not only as friends and kinsfolk."[42] Additionally, Philo also had some skepticism of the value that people placed on their lineage.[43] In fact, he rebukes those who "spring from great houses" and boast in the "splendour of their race" but unfortunately do not exemplify the nobility of their ancestors.[44] Those who do not live a virtuous life, as he argues, "destroy ancestral prestige" and "quench all the glory which illumines the family."[45] For Philo, what mattered more than the nobility of one's lineage was a virtuous life.

However, there were limits and boundaries to the full inclusion of gentiles. Philo remarks that the Jews welcome anyone but are zealous for the temple and will not allow non-Jews to enter its inner courts.[46] He also claims that gentiles are gladly received into the Jewish community but are not allowed to be fully included until the third generation. Philo states:

> If any of them should wish to pass over into the Jewish community, they must not be spurned with an unconditional refusal as children of enemies, but be so far favoured that the third generation is invited to the congregation and made partakers in the divine revelations,

---

41. Philo, *On the Virtues* 102.
42. Philo, *On the Virtues* 103.
43. Philo, *On the Virtues* 187.
44. Philo, *On the Virtues* 197.
45. Philo, *On the Virtues* 191, 206.
46. Philo remarks, "Still more abounding and peculiar is the zeal of them all for the temple, and the strongest proof of this is that death without appeal is the sentence against those of other races who penetrate into its inner confines. For the outer are open to everyone wherever they come from" (*On Embassy to Gaius* 211).

to which also the native born, whose lineage is beyond reproach, are rightfully admitted.[47]

Philo's quote shows a sincere acceptance of gentiles, yet he also emphasizes that gentiles are distinct from those who are "native born" with a "lineage beyond reproach." In other words, birth and lineage serve as key identity markers that differentiate gentile converts from Jews. And although Philo's positive comments about gentile converts were welcomed, they were not universal. As we reviewed in rabbinic thought, converts were still racially different because they lack the lineage connection with a Jewish ancestry. The convert may have the same legal status and social acceptance, but the convert is not regarded on equal terms with someone who is truly Jewish by birth.

THE SPIRIT'S SUBVERSION OF ESTEEMED LINEAGES

As we can notice thus far, having the right lineage was important in the ancient world. Being in the right lineage granted one access, privileges, and even responsibilities. Such individuals also had the power to determine whether one was included in or excluded from a community. Yet, overall, these networks drew relational boundaries of racial groups. With these insights in mind, we can now turn to the primary question and bring this chapter to a fitting conclusion—that is, what does it mean to be born of the Spirit?

When Jesus tells Nicodemus that it is necessary for him to be "born again," the repeated emphasis on being "born" challenges Nicodemus's understanding of racial relations, including the rights and privileges that come with being born into a Jewish ancestry. The Spirit is now the one who grants a new lineage, one who destabilizes all privileged race relations, kinship groups, and myths of racial origins. Respected racial lineages become insignificant in comparison to the new lineage granted through the birthing activity of the Spirit. This is not to eradicate and consider racial identity

---

47. Philo, *On the Virtues* 108.

Marking One's Birth by the Spirit (John 3)

superfluous. Instead, our disparate racial identities are bonded through the common birthing experience of the Spirit. By rooting one's lineage within the divine Spirit, all privileges that come from being born into a particular ancestry become neutralized.

For the readers of John's Gospel who are observing, and still debating, their relationship with the Jews and Jewish Christian communities in the late first century, the argument on the need to be "born of the Spirit" had major racial significance. In the ancient world, not having genealogical relations to a community meant that one held neither the territorial right to common space such as the kingdom of God nor the ability to justify one's inclusion as an equal member on all terms. Converts were recognized as members of inferior status because of their lack of genealogical relations to the Jewish ancestry. Thus, if new members from a non-Jewish lineage were filling the synagogue, this would have brought a new challenge to the old way of thinking that only lineage-linked Jews had access to the promises of God. In Jesus's conversation with Nicodemus, we are therefore hearing not only a dialogue about the Spirit's role in birthing new members into the kingdom of God but also an argument of racial inclusion based on the Spirit.

This helps us recognize that an appeal to being born of the Spirit presents a challenge to those who held genealogical values and boundaries. To champion the need to be "born again" by the Spirit is a challenge to those who uphold and maintain systems of privileged lineage or racial superiority. Since membership in the kingdom of God is not based upon one's racial lineage, the Johannine community needs to be one that has an ever-expansive and inclusive understanding of what it means to be and call one another a child of God. This also means that members should not have trepidation in admitting those who have questionable racial identities—including foreigners. Membership into the kingdom of God through the Spirit eradicates the privileges and pride of being a descendant of Abraham. More specifically, views and practices that foster xenophobia and racial exclusion because of one's racial ancestry are practices contrary to the Spirit's birthing activity of inclusion. Xenophobia, racism, and exclusion are not merely wrong for morality's sake, but they are the anti-pneumatic spirits that roam the earth and bring about division and animosity toward those whom the Spirit has embraced through a new birth.

4

Accessing the Space of the Spirit (John 4)

IN JOHN 4, JESUS travels with his disciples from Judea to Galilee. They, however, do not walk alongside the Jordan River. Instead, they travel through the region of Samaria. Was this a detour or simply the route Jesus needed to take? The route through Samaria might have been shorter but involved going through an area that did not historically have good relations with the Jewish people. Though we are not sure why Jesus decides to take this route, the Gospel writer insists that this was necessary (v. 4). While on the journey, Jesus sits near a well in the Samaritan town of Sychar. His disciples have just gone into the city to buy food, leaving him by himself. So, Jesus, tired as he is from the journey, asks this unnamed Samaritan woman who happens to be there for some water to drink (v. 7).

Now, this story in John 4 is intriguing for many reasons. First, the encounter reflects a betrothal narrative common in the Old Testament. Notice how many times that a man meets another woman at a well. Isaac, Jacob, and Moses—they all found their significant other through an encounter at a well.[1] This episode

---

1. Eslinger, "Wooing of the Woman," 166–68. Allusions to betrothal scenes include Gen 24:10–61; 29:1–20; Exod 2:15–21.

in John's Gospel continues a similar plot with Jesus meeting the Samaritan woman. However, there is a major twist in the narrative. The dynamics of this story differ. We never really know the identity of this woman besides her racial and marital background. Additionally, there is a crossing of gender boundaries that were typically upheld in the ancient world.[2] It was not normal for Jewish men and Samaritan women to socialize—and especially to be alone together. Further, this story ventures into a conversation about the coming prophet, discusses Jesus's messianic identity, and deals with issues that stem from their contrasting claims on temple worship. Jesus has a dense conversation with this unnamed Samaritan woman.

Though this chapter will not dive into all the topics mentioned above, we will specifically focus on Jesus's teaching on the Spirit and the racial implications of their conversation in John 4:23–24. This will also include how the discussion about the Spirit emerges in response to the Samaritan woman's remarks about the appropriate place to worship God, a claim that runs counter to the Jewish emphasis on Jerusalem. Let us start with Jesus's response to the Samaritan woman's view of worship:

> Jesus said to her, "Believe me, woman, an hour is coming when you all will worship the Father neither in this mountain nor in Jerusalem. You all worship what you do not know, we worship what we do know, because salvation is from the Jews. But an hour is coming and now is here, when the true worshipers will worship the Father in Spirit and in truth, for even the Father seeks these who worship him. God is Spirit, and those who worship him, must worship in Spirit and truth." (John 4:21–24)

Notice in Jesus's response how he puts forth a new place of worship, one not only reflective of God's identity but also one that

---

2. Philo reflects the ancient gender stereotype and division in public and private spaces when he remarks that the woman is most suitable for the indoor life. In Philo, *Spec.* 3 169–71, 178, males and females are believed to have two different types of souls. See Xenophon, *Oeconomicus* 7.19–7.21; Hierocles, *On Duties* 4.28.21. Ben Sira also warns males of spending time with women alone, especially if they are married (Sir 9:9; 42:12).

Accessing the Space of the Spirit (John 4)

emphasizes the importance of the Spirit and truth. But how do Jesus's teachings about the Spirit relate to race? Is Jesus simply talking about a form of spiritual worship? Even more, what does race have to do with mountains?

Before we answer these questions, I want to point out a not-so-obvious aspect of this conversation. We must keep in mind that Jesus's response is not rejecting the Samaritan woman's racial identity and the tradition of her people through his insistence that worship on mountains will not matter. Instead, what we find is that Jesus is speaking to all Jews, Samaritans, and even readers of the Gospel. As will be argued in this chapter, he urges them to recognize that worship in the Spirit is characterized primarily by the rejection of racially hostile behaviors that their mountains have come to symbolize. Since God is Spirit, we must worship God in this reality of truth. What is this truth? In essence, that our temples seated on mountains are insufficient to contain God. They are unable to fully hold God's presence and have only become inaccessible spaces for people.

This chapter proceeds by setting the dialogue in context, one we must understand in light of the two contrasting perspectives on worship—Jewish and Samaritan. Central to this chapter's argument is the claim that Jesus's dialogue about worship can be understood only when the historical factors of racial hostility, lineage purity, and competing religious temples shape how we read the response to the Samaritan woman. As such, I explore the Samaritan people's racial identity as a distinct group that differed from the Jewish people to help us understand why the Samaritan woman wanted to talk about worshiping God on a mountain. Last, I conclude with some observations on John's view of the Spirit and how this dialogue expands our understanding of racial identity and race relations.

The Spirit in John's Gospel
READING THE WORSHIP DIALOGUE IN CONTEXT

The dialogue within the context of John 4 can be read in reference to the true worshipers, both in the present and future (vv. 21–23). This call for true worshipers does not make irrelevant one's racial identity. Jesus is talking about real people in real locations with their particular histories and layered identities. Although some may see the woman as a symbolic figure,[3] the story focuses particular attention on the Samaritan woman's personal life, the community she represents, and readers aware of racial tensions with the Jews. All these aspects are brought together in this dialogue, and the reader is alerted to them when the Samaritan woman reminds Jesus of his "Jewish" identity and how Jews have no dealings with the Samaritans. John even helps provide further clarification by stating, "For Jews and Samaritans do not associate with one another" (v. 9). This is a point that scholars on the Gospel of John have also observed.[4] Throughout the story, the readers hear the differences between Jesus and the woman, not only in terms of gender and race but with respect to their theological traditions. They did not associate with one another because, as I explain in the next section, the Jews typically classified the Samaritans as a completely different racial group.[5]

---

3. Sandra Schneiders views the woman as a symbolic figure representing the Samaritan element in the Johannine community (*Revelatory Text*, 180–99).

4. The term συγχράομαι, translated as "associate" or "having dealings with," is found only here in John's Gospel. It does not appear anywhere else in the New Testament. Scholars note that the enmity between the two groups would have been common knowledge for the first-century reader. See Bultmann, *Gospel of John*, 178; Brown, *Gospel According to John*, 1:170; Barrett, *St. John*, 194–95; Keener, *Gospel of John*, 598–601. Morris, however, is unsure of how the Jews viewed each other, given that the disciples venture into the city to buy food and thus show no reservation with Samaritans (*Gospel According to John*, 229).

5. Jesus in Matthew's Gospel does not consider Samaritans as part of the "lost sheep" of Israel (Matt 10:4–5). Likewise, when Jesus is rejected by the Samaritans in Luke's Gospel, the disciples are eager to call fire from heaven to consume them (Luke 9:51–56). Jesus describes the Samaritan leper who was healed a "foreigner" (Luke 17:16–18). The same term Luke uses (ἀλλογενὴς)

Accessing the Space of the Spirit (John 4)

Yet the conversation gets personal between Jesus and the Samaritan woman. The Samaritan woman comes to know Jesus's identity as a prophet when he talks about her marriage history, but when Jesus calls the woman to bring her husband, she does not immediately leave the well as Jesus bids. Instead, she draws Jesus's attention to Mount Gerizim (John 4:20). This reference to Mount Gerizim, as some suppose, may appear as an attempt to defer further discussions about her marriages.[6] We can, however, entertain the possibility that the Samaritan woman sensed the liberty to bring to Jesus's attention a point of bitter conflict between their racial communities, given that he demonstrated himself to be a prophet.[7] She presents Jesus with a dilemma about the proper place of worship. In fact, the Samaritan people anticipated a coming prophet as promised in Deut 18:18.[8]

According to Samaritan tradition, they believed that a prophet would arrive at Mount Gerizim and restore the worship of God in the tradition of a priest like Moses.[9] The Samaritan people anticipated not a Davidic Messiah but a prophet who would have a priestly role and restore the tabernacle worship. This was the essential characteristic of Samaritanism: its concept of a priestly religion founded on the Pentateuch with its focus on Mount Gerizim. Since Jesus was a prophet, she supposes Jesus is the most qualified person to reveal God's will and to address this theological problem that had severed the relations between Jews and Samaritans throughout the decades.

---

is also found in the LXX to describe foreigners forbidden to enter the temple complex (Jer 28:50–51; Ezek 44:7–9).

6. Morris, *Gospel According to John*, 236.

7. Jean Kim insists that the Samaritan woman has been stereotyped as an immoral woman without the reader knowing why she had many husbands. She proposes that the colonization of Samaria and victimization of women during periods of war provide another alternative view that does not negatively portray the Samaritan woman as immoral. See Kim, "Korean Feminist Reading."

8. Meeks, *Prophet-King*, 216–57.

9. Bowman, *Samaritan Problem*, 31.

What is often absent in a popular understanding of this conversation is how much it is embedded with tense racial histories and differing religious traditions between Jews and Samaritans. The woman's concern for her racial community is made evident when she states, "Our fathers worshipped on this mountain" (John 4:20). Who are her "fathers"? She is talking about her ancestors and the lineage to which she belongs. Notice how the Samaritan woman contrasts her ancestral practice with the Jewish people, who insist that Jerusalem is the proper place of worship. We must note that the conversation on worship begins when the Samaritan woman challenges Jesus as a Jewish prophet. In some sense, she presents the current state of affairs and, in a subtle way, reminds Jesus about the social and political history between Jews and Samaritans. She has an element of defense in recalling where her ancestors worshiped. One cannot help but recognize that embedded within her statement is a memory of violence and trauma that has resulted in the formation of a different worshiping community—people separated not only geographically but also religiously and racially. Even more, in bringing this to Jesus's attention she points not to a standing temple on Mount Gerizim but to its ruins, the scars that Jesus's Jewish ancestors had inflicted upon her Samaritan people.

To understand the Samaritan woman's boldness to confront Jesus about Mount Gerizim and the proper place to worship God, we must do justice to the violence and segregation experienced by the Samaritans. In a brief review of Samaritan identity and history within the next section, I highlight the importance of Mount Gerizim for the Samaritan people and how their mountain emerged as a bitter point of tension with the Jewish people.

SAMARITAN IDENTITY AND RACE

Who are the Samaritan people? Samaritan and Jewish people had a long history of racial tension and division. Interestingly, the people who lived in Samaria did not consider themselves "Samaritans." Gary Knoppers makes this point when he insists that the designation "Samaritan" is largely shunned, given that the people in this

Accessing the Space of the Spirit (John 4)

region prefer to call themselves northern Israelites or Samarian Israelites.[10] The story of the Samaritan people as a distinct racial group emerged after the northern Israelites who lived in Samaria were exiled by the Assyrian Empire. In the Old Testament, there is an anti-Samaritan tradition that emerges from 2 Kgs 17:24–41, which describes the resettlement of Samaria with a new people unrelated to the Jewish people. Josephus, a Jewish historian during the Roman Empire, remarks that the term "Samaritan" is a Greek translation of people who resettled the land of Samaria. The people who resettled the region were from Persia and called Cuthians.[11] Josephus insists that the Samaritans were distinct from the Jewish people and utilized their lineage relations only when it benefited them—and were therefore inferior to the Jews.[12] This suggests that throughout time, there was racial intermixing, since the Assyrian captivity of the region exiled the original Jewish inhabitants of the land. The Samaritan people, as Josephus proposes, had no legitimate racial relations with the original Jewish ancestors.

Why does this matter? In the ancient world there was an assumption that groups of people were either inferior or superior to others. Yes, this is a racial ideology that eerily sounds familiar. However, the ancients did not base this ideology on skin color the way we do today. They focused on other factors such as lineage and culture. Benjamin Isaac remarks that the idea that people of superior quality should be of pure lineages without a mixture of foreign elements among their ancestors was a common conviction.[13] This idea is found most notably in the writings of the Greeks. It was Plato who used a myth of pure lineage and national identity to justify

---

10. Knoppers, *Jews and the Samaritans*, 15.

11. Josephus, *Jewish Antiquities* 9.288–9.291. Josephus also states regarding the Samaritans, "When they see the Jews prospering, [they] call them their kinsmen, on the ground that they are descended from Joseph and are related to them through their origin from him, but, when they see the Jews in trouble, they say that they have nothing whatever in common with them nor do these have any claim of friendship or race, and they declare themselves to be aliens of another race" (9.291).

12. Josephus, *Jewish Antiquities* 9.288–9.291; 11.341–11.345.

13. Isaac, *Invention of Racism*, 109.

a love of freedom and a hatred of foreigners.[14] Plato assumed that a mixed population would bring immense deterioration to the native people of the land.[15] As such, maintaining a pure lineage was an important duty for many racial groups. It shaped marriage preferences—that is, who you could or could not marry. It also placed value on descendants and their offspring—the more one married within one's racial group, the more legitimate and superior one's descendants would be. Last, it justified the separation or rejection of immigrants, who would bring a threat to their lineage.

Strikingly, Josephus refers to Plato's claim when he defends the Jewish conviction that they should not intermarry or socialize with gentiles. He draws from Plato in stating that he "took precautions to prevent foreigners from mixing with them at random" and sought to "keep the state pure and confined to law-abiding citizens."[16] Josephus further notes that Jews were not the only ones ambivalent toward foreigners. He remarks that this practice "is common to all, and shared not only by Greeks, but by Greeks of the highest reputation."[17] Josephus uses these Greek suspicions of foreigners and emphasis on lineage purity to justify the anti-social behavior that is charged against the Jews, while at the same time trying to propose that Jews are receptive of foreigners.[18] When we hear the conversation between Jesus and the Samaritan woman from this perspective, we must incorporate the racial ideology of lineages. This idea not only explains the racial animosity and suspicion of the Samaritan people, but it also clarifies why there was racial segregation and rejection of the Samaritan claim that they were legitimate worshipers who descended from Israel. Having a mixed lineage fostered the assumption that the Samaritans were inferior, polluted, and should be avoided since they did not preserve their genealogy from their Jewish ancestor, Manasseh.

14. Plato, *Menexenus* 245c–d.
15. Plato, *Leg.* 12.949e–950a.
16. Josephus, *Against Apion* 2.257.
17. Josephus, *Against Apion* 2.259.
18. Josephus, *Against Apion* 2.258–2.259.

Accessing the Space of the Spirit (John 4)

RELEVANCE OF MOUNTAINS IN WORSHIP

How then does race relate to worshiping in Jerusalem or on Mount Gerizim? To put it simply, we need to understand Jesus's dialogue about the Spirit in light of the history of violence, racial perceptions of lineage purity, and worship disagreements between the Jews and Samaritans. Let us begin by exploring how Jesus responds to the Samaritan woman's assertion. Jesus states, "You all worship what you do not know; we worship what we know" (John 4:22). Jesus's response defends the Jewish people by noting that they are worshiping a God who they know, given that salvation has come from them.[19] Again, the conversation within vv. 20–24 is best understood not only between two individuals but between distinct communities who hold contrasting claims about worship and their knowledge of God. But Jesus does not stop there in v. 22 with those statements. If he did, he would sound like someone who simply sided with the Jewish people and viewed all others as ignorant of God. Instead, Jesus wants to move past these points of disagreement and mentions the possibility of their future inclusion, which will not be limited to a particular mountain.

What was Jesus's solution? Simply put, that worship of God must be done in the Spirit. When the worship of God is grounded in the Spirit, it does not suggest that one's racial identity is irrelevant. Jesus is still a Jew and does not deny his Jewishness. Even more, Jesus and the apostles continued to travel to the temple for worship and to maintain the priority of Jerusalem.[20] Though the Jewish and Samaritan temples had been destroyed before the Gospel was composed, aspirations toward rebuilding the temple did not diminish.[21] People still worship in sacred spaces. Worship

---

19. Bultmann raises the possibility that the plural refers to the Johannine community, who understands how to give true worship (*Gospel of John*, 189–90n6).

20. As noticed with Jesus, Paul, and the apostles, the Jerusalem temple still played an important role in the early Christian community. See also Fuglseth, *Johannine Sectarianism*, 128–36; Acts 2:46; 3:1; 5:42; 21:26–30; 24:17; 24:18; 25:8; 26:21; Heb 8:5; 9:8–10.

21. As noticed during the Bar Kokhba Revolt (132–35 CE) and in

never occurs in a nonspatial location or by people with no racial identities. The response Jesus gives the Samaritan woman should not be viewed as an argument that race or space does not matter. Additionally, Jesus's response to the Samaritan woman about the irrelevance of sacred mountains is not to disregard the racial identity, trauma, or violence that the Samaritans experienced when Mount Gerizim was desecrated by the Greeks and destroyed by the Hasmoneans. Jesus is pointing to new attitudes and practices that shape how Jews and Samaritans should view each other, especially since the deteriorating relations between the Samaritans and Jews continued well outside of Judea under Roman rule and were etched in the rabbinic tradition.[22] Instead, Jesus's statements include larger implications about racial exclusion. The Samaritans and Johannine readers would have identified with and felt what it meant to be told that they had no right to access the presence of God because they lacked a certain racial identity. To gloss over these implications and propose a reading of the story that minimizes the issues of racial suspicion and violence against cultural identity markers such as a temple is to miss the full effect of Jesus's statement.

More importantly, Jesus is pointing to the uselessness of upholding segregationist claims and racial boundaries that our mountains or "churches" have come to symbolize. Claiming that Mount Gerizim is important, or the temple in Jerusalem, has led only to destruction and the prohibition of the racially other. We must note that the Samaritans were not able to rebuild their temple[23] and on one occasion secretly entered Jerusalem to scatter human bones before the temple colonnades.[24] This defiled the Jerusalem temple and led to its immediate temporary closure. On another occasion, the Samaritans also killed Galileans who were on their way to

---

Benediction 14, *Shmoneh Esreh*; Fuglseth argues that positive attitudes of the temple by the first Christians indicates that the temple was not abandoned even if it was theologically surpassed (*Johannine Sectarianism*, 117–85).

22. See m. Ber. 7.1; 8.8; m. Šeb. 8.10; m. Nid. 4.1.
23. Knoppers, *Jews and the Samaritans*, 219.
24. Josephus, *Jewish Antiquities* 18.29–18.30.

Accessing the Space of the Spirit (John 4)

worship in Jerusalem, only to have the Judeans retaliate by setting nearby Samaritan villages on fire.[25] Josephus reminds us that there were conflicts between Jews and Samaritans over worship in Egypt on several occasions,[26] with one event leading to the execution of Samaritans.[27] The Samaritans were not permitted to enter the Jerusalem temple and were left to mourn the ruins of their sacred mountain with the aspiration to once again worship God.

The place of worship was a focal point of contention, and at the same time, the entrance requirements to the most sacred spaces within the temple were based on one's racial and gender identities. Temples represented and testified about the god the people worshiped. Different geographical regions were known for their temples. They reflected one's racial identity and the history of the community's relationship with their god. Even more, the Jerusalem temple prohibited non-Jews from entering its sacred space. Archeologists have unearthed an inscription that dates to the first century; this inscription was installed near the Jerusalem temple and warned foreigners from entering the inner court of the temple, reading, "No foreigner is to enter within the balustrade and forecourt around the sacred precinct. Whoever is caught will himself be responsible for (his) consequent death."[28] Josephus mentions this warning sign that prohibited non-Jews from entering the sacred space of the Jerusalem temple.[29] Philo remarks that the outer court of the temple was available for all people; only the "inner confines" were excluded.[30] In fact, the apostle Paul was arrested for supposedly bringing Greeks into the temple, thus violating this prohibition (Acts 21:26–30). Related to John 4, we can notice that

---

25. Josephus: *Jewish War* 2.234–2.240; *Jewish Antiquities* 20.118–20.121.
26. Josephus, *Jewish Antiquities* 12.10.
27. Josephus, *Jewish Antiquities* 13.74–13.79.
28. Cotton et al., *Jerusalem*, 43.
29. Josephus: *Jewish War* 5.193–5.195; 6.126; *Jewish Antiquities* 12.145; 15.417. See also Orian, "Purpose of the Balustrade."
30. Philo states, "Death without appeal is the sentence against those of other races who penetrate into its inner confines. For the outer are open to everyone wherever they come from" (*On Embassy to Gaius* 212).

temples were no small matter. They were central points of violence if their sacred spaces were violated and the source of segregation between Jews, Samaritans, and all foreigners.

One must detect that the conversation between Jesus and the Samaritan woman was not just about spiritual worship. The interaction had ramifications that could continue violence and racial attitudes of superiority and exclusion, or it could reduce these prospects. What we read is a powerful argument that points to the fact that God as Spirit means that the realm of the Spirit is the most important location of our worship. To enter this realm of the Spirit, one must reject the practices and perspectives that result in racial-political animosity and violence. Barring people from sacred spaces or destroying temples has no place within the people of God. Those who insist that mountains matter are those bent on destroying one another's sacred spaces. Those who believe they are racially superior are the ones who justify practices of exclusion and discrimination through temple boundaries and worship segregation.

As a result, there is no justification for the prejudicial views that characterized Jewish and Samaritan racial relations. By pointing to the realm of the Spirit in which worship must occur, Jesus also reveals that discriminatory practices, perspectives, and symbols based on racial supremacist ideologies are in themselves contrary to the work of the Spirit. Racism and racial exclusion are anti-pneumatic. Jesus's insistence that worship is in the Spirit challenges those who used race to segregate, exclude, and condone temple violence.

THEOLOGY OF RACE AND WORSHIP

Overall, this also makes us wonder how the readers of the Gospel, also known as the Johannine community, would have understood this story during the late first century in the city of Ephesus.[31] They might have heard these passages in light of an ever-growing rift

---

31. R. Brown, *Community of Beloved Disciple*, 17–78; Eusebius, *Hist. eccl.* 3.18.1; 3.20.11; 3.23.4–3.23.19; 3.39; 5.24.

between Jews, Greeks, and Samaritans in emerging Christianity.[32] Jesus's discussion on the Spirit presents the Johannine community with a new way of looking at worship and the role of temples held by people. Jesus's insistence that worship is in the Spirit moves the Samaritan woman and readers into a new understanding of racial relationships and competing religious claims. Since God is Spirit and acts toward humanity in Spirit, then all worship toward God and relations with one another must no longer be bent on the privileging of temples or the maintenance of racial segregation. Jesus's insistence that worship must be in the Spirit suggests that believers must recognize that institutions of national identity that alienate people hold no place within the worshiping community. Instead, Jesus's statements include larger implications toward the racial identity and temple segregation that the Samaritan woman and the Johannine readers would have identified and experienced. Again, to gloss over these implications and propose a reading of the story that minimizes the issues of racial superiority and violence is to miss the fuller understanding of Jesus's statement.

But what does it mean to worship? We have been discussing this topic but have yet to define it. The term "worship" comes from the Greek word προσκυνέω, which means to "fall down" or "prostrate oneself."[33] This term occurs on eleven occasions within the Gospel of John, with most mentions occurring in this dialogue alone.[34] The next time the term appears is when a blind man who was miraculously healed encounters Jesus (John 9:38). Originally, the blind man who experienced this miracle had not known that Jesus healed him. Not until the blind man encounters and sees Jesus for the first time does he confess his faith in Jesus and worship him. The final mention of this term occurs when some Greeks arrive in Jerusalem and desire to worship God at the feast (12:20). The Greeks are traveling migrants. While in Jerusalem, these

---

32. John Christopher Thomas points out that the Fourth Gospel seems to reflect an accurate knowledge of emerging attitudes toward the Samaritans (*Spirit of New Testament*, 137–41).

33. Heinrich Greeven, "προσκυνέω," *TDNT* 6:759.

34. John 4:20–24 (nine mentions); 9:38; 12:20.

Greeks hear about Jesus and desire to see him, but the Gospel does not reveal if they eventually do so.

The Gospel of John expands our notion of who is worthy of our worship, who can properly worship, and where we can worship. In this sense, Jesus's dialogue with the Samaritan woman serves as an initial attempt to center the proper place and person of worship through a pneumatic perspective. Samaritans and Jews no longer need to consider themselves as being the only ones who practice the true form of worship that the Father seeks. Since the worship of God is done in the Spirit, only the Spirit has the right to reject worshipers and also is free to inhabit the realm of the worshiper. Furthermore, since the worship of God must be done in the Spirit, no group can enter the realm of the Spirit and still hold onto claims of racial exclusion or engage in border patrolling sacred spaces. The worshipers whom God the Father seeks are those whose worship makes space for the excluded other. True worship in the Spirit manifests itself with racial inclusion.

5

New Disciples in the Diaspora (John 7)

WHEN JESUS IS AT the Feast of Tabernacles in Jerusalem, he gives a statement on the last day of the festival to all those attending this celebratory event: "If anyone is thirsty, let him come to me and drink. The one who believes in me, as the Scripture said, from his innermost being will flow rivers of living water" (John 7:37–38). The Scripture Jesus refers to is difficult to find. There are no passages in the Old Testament that discuss the flowing of living water from the innermost being of a person. However, the writer of John's Gospel elaborates on the meaning of Jesus's words by clarifying, "He said this about the Spirit, whom those who believed in him were to receive, for the Spirit was not yet, because Jesus had not been glorified" (v. 39). The writer helps explain what Jesus was talking about. It was not literal water but the giving of the Spirit after his death and resurrection.

Why would Jesus invite the attendees of this festival to receive the Spirit if the Spirit could be given only after his death? If we consider Jesus's statements about the Spirit in isolation, disconnected from the context of John 7, it might seem confusing. It appears as though Jesus stands in Jerusalem and shouts to the crowds about receiving the Spirit in a metaphorical manner. So, on the one hand, Jesus invites all those who are thirsty to come to him for a drink and places himself as the source of satisfaction. But on the other hand, if anyone had taken Jesus up on his offer, they would have had to wait till the resurrection to receive the Spirit. How did the people respond? No one really approaches Jesus. Instead, those who heard Jesus proclaim these words call him a prophet and Messiah (vv. 40–41). They debate among themselves his identity and whether the Messiah would arise from Galilee.

Jesus's invitation to drink of living water is one of the earliest references to the giving of the Holy Spirit. Since the writer provides an explanation of Jesus's statement, this leads us to recognize that the ones who fully understand Jesus's invitation are the readers. And they, living in a multiracial and multicultural world, would resonate deeply with this invitation. Since this story is written with the readers in mind, the real question we must ask ourselves is the following: How would the multiracial readers in John's church hear Jesus's invitation to receive the Spirit? As I will argue in this chapter, the readers would come to recognize that Jesus—not a temple or a geographical location—is the source of the Spirit. As such, the giving of the Spirit is not hindered by any boundary but available for anyone who dares to approach him.

THE FEAST OF TABERNACLES

Before we go much further, however, I want to briefly unpack the significance of the festival. Its origins are attributed to Abraham, but it emerges as a celebration of the wilderness experience when the Hebrews lived in temporary shelters.[1] We find in the Old Testament various details about the feast. It lasted for eight days (Lev 23:36),[2] reenacted the wilderness experience through the construction and dwelling in temporary shelters (v. 42),[3] involved

---

1. Jub. 16:21–31; Lev 23:33–43.
2. Philo, *On the Special Laws* 2.211.
3. Philo, *On the Special Laws* 2.206.

a public reading of the law (Deut 31:10–13),[4] included daily sacrifices (Lev 23:36; Num 29:12–28), and required rest from labor (Lev 23:35). According to Josephus, this festival was the "most holy and most eminent feast."[5] It reminded the Jewish people of the Lord's deliverance of the Hebrews from Egypt. Philo, in fact, adds that the festival provided a time to "remember one's poverty, and in an hour of glory to recollect the days of one's disgrace, and at a season of peace to think upon the dangers that are past."[6] Celebrating this festival was very important for the Jewish people. There is even a warning to those who did not celebrate this feast. Zechariah claims that God would withhold rain from their fields, even if they lived in Egypt or other distant locations (Zech 14:16–19).

Later rabbinic literature enhances our understanding of what the Jewish people did during this festival. The temple priest would perform a water- and wine-pouring libation. Water was drawn from the pool of Siloam in a golden pitcher and brought to the temple. The people would follow the priests who carried the water to the entrance of the temple courtyard in celebration (m. Sukkah 4:1). This procession was a joyful experience with music and the reading of Isa 12:3, which states, "You will joyously draw water from the springs of salvation" (m. Sukkah 4:9–10; 5:1).[7] It is within this festival of remembering and celebrating the desert wilderness experience that Jesus makes a proclamation about living water. Those attending the festival would connect Jesus's statements with their ancestor's wilderness experience. They would agree that water is important for one's survival in the extreme conditions of the desert. But Jesus claims something much more that goes beyond the festival. He claims to be the one who provides living water that will emerge from within one's own belly. This does not make sense

---

4. Josephus *Jewish Antiquities* 3.244–3.245; 4.209; 11.154–11.157.
5. Josephus, *Jewish Antiquities* 8.100.
6. Philo, *On the Special Laws* 2.208.
7. Bruce Grigsby points to rabbinic texts that describe the expectations of rain upon those who are spiritually dry (Pesiq. Rab. 52) and the eschatological hope for water flowing from the temple (t. Sukkah 3.3–12). See Grigsby, "If Any Man Thirsts."

on a literal level, so the writer of John's Gospel explains that Jesus is talking about the Spirit.

GROWING TENSION AT THE FESTIVAL

Although this joyful festival serves as the ceremonial context of Jesus's proclamation on the Spirit, his experience in Jerusalem is nowhere near celebratory. The tone of the chapter is noticeably polemical with various hostile characters moving in and out of the scenes. Furthermore, the chapter begins with division within Jesus's own family and ends with rejection from those within his own racial community. In fact, the writer explains that Jesus was intentionally avoiding Judea because his own Jewish people desired to kill him (7:1). As the festival draws near, Jesus's brothers urge him to leave Galilee with his disciples in order to reveal himself to the world (vv. 2–9). This request to leave Galilee and emerge in the "public" scene is not prompted with Jesus's benefit in mind. The Gospel writer mentions that Jesus's brothers "did not believe in him," and they assumed that Jesus wanted to regain his disciples (v. 5). Prior to the prompting of Jesus's brothers, Jesus had recently lost many disciples after his teaching about bread and eating his flesh in John 6:60–66. Jesus does not immediately leave for Jerusalem but continues to remain in Galilee until much later (v. 9).

When Jesus finally arrives in Jerusalem, he does not want his presence known (v. 10). The Jews, however, are looking for him and in a murmuring manner debate among themselves about whether he was a good man or leading the people astray (v. 12). This accusation that Jesus was "leading the people astray" reflects a legal charge of enticing others to worship foreign gods.[8] No one desires to publicly defend Jesus, because some had "fear of the Jews" (v. 13).[9] They sense that even though Jesus is in Jerusalem to

---

8. Martyn, *History and Theology*, 80–83; Jesus is called a deceiver in rabbinic literature (b. Sanh. 43a; b. Sotah 47a). See also Deut 13:1–6 LXX; Justin, *Dial.* 69.

9. This phrase "fear of the Jews" appears in the Gospel for the first time. It emerges later in John 9:22; 19:38; 20:19.

New Disciples in the Diaspora (John 7)

celebrate this festival, his life is in danger, and some within his own Jewish community want to kill him.

About halfway through the celebration week, Jesus finally makes his presence known to the people by teaching in the temple (vv. 14–31). During his teaching a confrontational dialogue occurs with some Jews who question the source of his teachings. In response, Jesus defends his teachings by stating that only those who resolve to do the will of God can discern the source of his teachings (v. 17). He makes it known that they not only fail to know the law but are also attempting to kill him (vv. 17–19). These Jews find this claim and his accusation absurd. They believe he is demonically possessed and ask him to expose those who want to kill him (v. 20). Their desire for clarification does not quell the tense dialogue. Jesus explains that some seek his death due to a miracle he previously performed on the Sabbath (vv. 21–24); he refers here to his healing of a paralytic man in Jerusalem (John 5:1–18).

The Gospel writer then turns to another group called the "Jerusalemites," who were not pilgrims of the festival but native residents of the city.[10] They recognize that Jesus's presence in Jerusalem places his life in danger because some seek to kill him (vv. 25–27). These Jerusalemites dialogue among themselves whether Jesus is truly the Messiah and conclude that since they know where he is from, he could not possibly be the expected one. They assumed that the Messiah's origins would be a mystery (v. 27).[11] Following their discussion, Jesus continues to teach in the temple and responds to the rumors about his origins (vv. 28–29). This time, he informs them that they do not know his origin because they do not know who sent him. The crowd immediately reacts by attempting to arrest him (v. 30). Although they fail, we also find that some people from the crowds believe in him. Some of the Pharisees who

---

10. Beasley-Murray, *John*, 110.

11. The assumption existed that no one would know the origins of the Messiah. For the possible origin of this secret Messiah tradition, see Justin, *Dial.* 8.4; 110.1; 1 En. 48:6; 62:7; 2 Esd 13:52. Other passages that point to the sudden appearance of the Messiah include Dan 9:25; Mal 3:1; 4 Ezra 7:28; 13:32; 2 Bar. 29:3.

overhear the crowd's discussion respond by sending officers to arrest Jesus (vv. 31–32).

During this escalating drama and these grave threats, Jesus tells the people that he will no longer be with them, and they will not be able to find him (vv. 33–34). The Jews are confused by Jesus's statement, and some interpret Jesus's claim as a desire to go among the Jews in the diaspora to teach the Greeks. They are unaware of what Jesus means about "going to a place where they cannot find him" and wonder why he would venture to another region where Greeks live (vv. 35–36). Why would some assume that Jesus is leaving to the Greeks? What could have prompted their assumption that a Jew would desire to travel to a Greek region? There is a growing hostility toward Jesus, beginning with his family and extending to his community. Racial hostility and kinship rejection permeate the dialogue and the context of the Feast of Tabernacles. This is supposed to be a celebratory week, but for Jesus, going to Jerusalem has only accelerated his imminent death and fomented a rejection from his own racial community.

Those within the story who hear Jesus's statement recognize that in light of the various rumors about his teaching, origin, and threat upon his life, leaving Jerusalem seems like a possible safe alternative. The readers of the narrative can realize here that some of Jesus's own racial community is turning against him. What was Jesus to do in light of this growing isolation and rejection from his own people? His only option is either to remain in Jerusalem and die or to leave for another racial community and region, which ironically would fulfill his brothers' request to "reveal himself to the world" (v. 4).

We can thus notice why Jesus's enigmatic statement about "going away" would lead the Jews in Jerusalem to wonder whether Jesus desired to leave to the Greeks in the diaspora (v. 35). Leaving Jerusalem to find new disciples among the Greeks would be the safest route, given the constant threat against Jesus's life, rejection from his family, and the pending threat of arrest. But we also must note that Jesus never travels into gentile regions within John's

Gospel.¹² So the question about Jesus gaining new disciples in the diaspora also has a prophetic sense to it. Can this be a subtle reference to the later Christian outreach to Greeks and other people? Rudolf Bultmann supposes that this Jewish accusation to leave to the Greeks has a sense of irony.¹³ But for irony to succeed, as Gail O'Day contends, the readers of this story must find the real meaning of the statement in and through the expressed meaning.¹⁴ In other words, as we read this story, we can notice that Jesus does not dismiss the accusation that he desires to go to the Greeks. Certainly, Jesus never travels to the Greeks within his public ministry, but much later in the Gospel story they do come to him (12:20–22). As we read, irony abounds. The accusation that Jesus wanted to travel to the Greeks, while intended as a critical comment, actually hints at the universal nature of Jesus's mission and eventual spreading of the gospel to the Greeks and other gentiles.

GREEK-JEWISH ETHNIC RELATIONS

What then are the implications in knowing that a Jewish teacher such as Jesus has an openness to teach the Greeks? How would a Greek audience perceive Jesus's silence when he is accused of desiring to venture into their region? John Collins reminds us that the Jews in the diaspora setting were not reluctant exiles but open to Hellenistic influences and culture and aspired to gain respect from the Greeks.¹⁵ This Jewish openness to Greek culture does not suggest that resistance and tensions were absent. In the history of Greek-Jewish relations, we find racial hostility and admiration alongside one another. The Jews were widely known for separating themselves from non-Jews, a practice viewed as a form of Greek social hatred. These accusations led Josephus to respond by claiming that the Jews have an openness to outsiders, including Greeks. He states:

12. Fernando Segovia notices that Jesus's public life revolves around Jerusalem ("Journey[s] of the Word").
13. Bultmann, *Gospel of John*, 309.
14. O'Day, *Revelation in Fourth Gospel*, 8.
15. Collins, *Between Athens and Jerusalem*, 5.

> We neither hate nor envy them. On the contrary, many of them have agreed to adopt our laws, of whom some have remained faithful, while others, lacking the necessary endurance, have again seceded.[16]

Collins admits that Judaism appeared to them as a strange religion, and they experienced occasional hostility due to social tensions and the distinctiveness of the Jewish religion.[17] Yet the conflicting tensions between positive and negative estimations of Judaism led to some measure of accommodation and acculturation.[18] Racial boundaries were certainly crossed in the diaspora. When these dividing walls were traversed, there was a sharing of intellectual capital and improved relations.

Although it is difficult to pin down the first encounter between Greeks and Jews, we know that since the time of Herodotus, the Greeks were aware of Jewish presence in the east. Herodotus mistakes them for "Syrian Palestinians" when he describes them as a group of people who learned the custom of circumcision from the Egyptians.[19] We also discover in Josephus's writings further testimony of contact between the Jews and the Greeks. Josephus believes that the Greeks were acquainted with Jewish people and utilized their writings in their works.[20] This includes Pythagoras, a man "ranked above all the philosophers," who was an admirer of Jewish institutions.[21] Josephus even submits that Pythagoras "introduced many points of Jewish law into his philosophy."[22] From Josephus's perspective, the Greeks were not only acquainted with the Jewish people but also had cross-cultural interactions that influenced Greek culture.

---

16. Josephus, *Against Apion* 2.123–2.124.
17. Collins, *Between Athens and Jerusalem*, 8–12.
18. Collins, *Between Athens and Jerusalem*, 25.
19. Herodotus, *Persian Wars* 2.104.
20. Josephus, *Against Apion* 1.161.
21. Josephus, *Against Apion* 1.162–1.163; Porphyry also quotes Antonius Diogenes, who claims that Pythagoras borrowed his knowledge of dreams from the Jews (*Vit. Pyth.* 1.11).
22. Josephus, *Against Apion* 1.165–1.166.

New Disciples in the Diaspora (John 7)

In fact, there is a legendary encounter between Aristotle and Jewish philosophers. While this story is quoted only by Josephus, it retells an encounter between Aristotle and a Jewish man. In this encounter, Aristotle states,

> It would take too long to repeat the whole story, but there were features in that man's character, at once strangely marvellous and philosophical, which merit description ... the man was a Jew of Coele-Syria. These people are descended from the Indian philosophers. The philosophers, they say, are in India called Calani, in Syria by the territorial name of Jews; for the district which they inhabit is known as Judaea. Their city has a remarkably odd name: they call it Hierusaleme. Now this man, who was entertained by a large circle of friends and was on his way down from the interior to the coast, not only spoke Greek, but had the soul of a Greek. During my stay in Asia, he visited the same places as I did, and came to converse with me and some other scholars, to test our learning. But as one who had been intimate with many cultivated persons, it was rather he who imparted to us something of his own.[23]

From Aristotle's perspective, the Jews were believed to be descendants of philosophers. The Jewish man whom Aristotle encounters had the soul of a Greek and was bilingual. He not only impresses Aristotle but is described in such a way that Aristotle sees his own people in him.

This is not the only time that the Greeks view the Jews as philosophical people. This esteemed view is also found in the writing of Porphyry, who quotes Theophrastus, a disciple of Aristotle. Theophrastus describes them as "a race of philosophers [who] converse with each other about divinity, and during the night they view the stars, turning their eyes to them and invoking God with prayers."[24] Another early view of the Jewish people is found by Hecataeus of Abdera, who praises Moses for his outstanding

---

23. Josephus, *Against Apion* 1.177–1.181.
24. Porphyry, "On Abstinence."

wisdom and courage.²⁵ This is all to say that the Jewish people are also portrayed as having an esteemed intellectual honor. In the writings of Aristotle, Porphyry, and others, the Greeks recognized the Jews for their wisdom that was analogous to Greek philosophy. Erich Gruen, in fact, argues that the Greeks were comfortable in ascribing to Jews conceptualizations that coincided with their own and including them within the Greek philosophical tradition.²⁶ He suggests that the mutual appropriations of cultures between the Jews and Greeks was not a diminution of their identity but an enhancement of it.²⁷ The claim that the Jews were to be regarded along the same philosophical intellectual heritage would have been an acclamation for the Jewish people who lived among the Greeks in the Roman world.

When we look to the evangelistic outreach of the early apostolic church, the Greeks were the first to receive the gospel message. Luke records that the first followers of Jesus in Antioch included both Jews and Greeks (Acts 11:20–21). In the cities of Iconium, Thessalonica, Athens, and Ephesus, many Greeks alongside the Jews came to faith in Jesus through the ministry of Paul.²⁸ Paul recognized that his desire to preach the gospel was for both "Jews and Greeks."²⁹ This further points out that relationship was not always hostile. We do find elements of mutual interest and openness to share and dialogue with one another.

RECEIVING THE SPIRIT THROUGH GREEK EYES

When we apply the Greek-Jewish relations to our reading of John 7:33–36, the charge that Jesus desired to "go to the Greeks" could

---

25. Diodorus, *Bib. hist.* 40.3. See also Hecataeus's remarks about a Jewish solider named Mosollamus. He is described as intelligent, robust, and a good bowman who accompanied Alexander the Great (Josephus, *Against Apion* 1.200–1.204).

26. Gruen, *Rethinking the Other*, 314.

27. Gruen, *Rethinking the Other*, 325.

28. Acts 14:1; 17:4, 17–34; 19:17–19.

29. Rom 1:14, 16; 1 Cor 1:22, 24; 10:32; 12:13; Gal 3:28; Col 3:11.

New Disciples in the Diaspora (John 7)

have been viewed in at least two ways. The Jewish crowd realizes that this would be the one place where Jesus could hide from the looming threat of death. They wonder if he wants to gain new disciples from among the Greeks. But in Jesus's failure to defend himself against this accusation, we find that he does not mind the claim of seeking disciples among the Greeks. So, from another perspective, this is also a way for the Gospel to demonstrate that Jesus, a "Jewish philosopher," had an openness to the Greeks. This sensitivity to the Greek outreach in John's Gospel underscores the importance of crossing racial barriers. It demonstrates that the message of the gospel is not restricted to only the Jews in Judea but has a much wider outreach to those whom one least expects.

On the final day of the festival, Jesus states, "If anyone is thirsty, let him come to me and drink. The one who believes in me, as the Scripture said, from his innermost being will flow rivers of living water" (v. 37). The call for "anyone" to approach him includes any person from within Jesus's own family and Jewish community. For the readers, it also includes the Greeks associated with Jesus's new mission. Between Jesus's invitation for anyone to approach him and the reaction of the Jews, we find the writer's interpretation of Jesus's words. The writer explains, "He said this about the Spirit, whom those who believed in him were to receive, for the Spirit was not yet, because Jesus had not been glorified" (v. 39).

As mentioned earlier, why would Jesus invite the thirsty to drink if the Spirit could be received only after his glorification? Jesus's invitation certainly cannot be understood from the perspective of the characters within the story. The characters struggle to find the meaning of Jesus's statement because they are confounded by his kinship origins and possible desire to go to the Greeks. The invitation is only properly understood from the perspective of the readers who live in a post-glorification period. Only they find the true meaning of Jesus's invitation through the Gospel writer's comments. And this meaning is cradled within a context of mounting pressure and rejection from one's own people, racial hostility, and racial boundary crossing. These racial aspects are easily discernible to the diaspora readers, because as racial members within

John's church, they, too, are familiar with the hostility and amicability that abounds between Greeks and Jews. As listeners of Jesus's words, observers of the ironic charge of going to the Greeks, and with the writer's explanation, they become the real people who Jesus invites.

So, what does the Spirit have to do with water? Or, more specifically, how does the phrase "from his innermost being will flow rivers of living water" (7:38) relate to the Spirit? Although there is no direct source to the scriptural reference, a strong association exists of water and Spirit that is attested throughout biblical literature. Jesus utilizes at least three possible scriptural themes in describing the giving of the Spirit. The first possible allusion is Exod 17:1–6 when the Hebrews are in the desert and grumble over the lack of water. In response, God instructs Moses to strike the rock at Horeb with his staff. Water flows from the rock in the presence of all the people. This divine intervention is described in Pss 78:15–16 and 105:41 as God giving the people abundant water like streams running down like a river.[30]

There is also the general association of the Spirit with water imagery. Joel 2:28 describes the Spirit as "poured out" on all flesh. A similar prophetic promise also appears in Isa 44:3, which reads, "I will pour water on the thirsty land, and streams on the dry ground; I will pour out my Spirit on your offspring, and my blessing on your descendants."[31] God also promises to cleanse the people from idolatry through the sprinkling of water. After this washing, God is going to give the people a new heart and place his Spirit within them (Ezek 36:25–27). Notice how the visible image of flowing water serves as a powerful metaphor for the giving of the Spirit. In fact, the prophet Isaiah mentions that God will refresh the dry land with water and give his Spirit to the descendants of Israel (44:3). The prophet reminds the people that they will no longer thirst, because God will lead them to springs of water (49:10). Isaiah has a similar invitation to the thirsty who lack the resources to become nourished (55:1). Drinking water and

30. Menken, "Origin of Old Testament Quotation."
31. See also Neh 9:20; Ezek 36:25–27; Zech 12:10.

experiencing a satisfaction from thirst express the reception of God's salvation and restoration. This is another possible meaning of Jesus's description of the Spirit.

Yet, there is something more with this water imagery. The third allusion is found in prophetic literature, which associates the water imagery with the temple. The prophet Ezekiel reveals a vision of rivers flowing from its foundation and bringing life to all the creatures, nourishing the vegetation of the land, and filling the oceans. The water that gushes forth from the Jerusalem temple indiscriminately provides life to various parts of the earth (Ezek 47:1–12). This is similar to other promises that describe water flowing from the temple, bringing life, or cleansing the people from their sins and impurities.[32] Water symbolizes a spiritual renewal, a cleansing from sin, reception of wisdom, salvation, and even life.[33] As we can notice, the water imagery is used to describe the renewal and refreshment that the people of God will receive from the Jerusalem temple. This is also why water becomes a vivid metaphor associated with the water pouring libations during the Festival of Tabernacles.

Overall, in the passages reviewed we can notice how they depict the Spirit with the imagery of water and the common human experience of thirst. This is a powerful metaphor that recurs throughout the Bible, making the connection between the Spirit and water a natural one. Applied to the Gospel's context, when Jesus cries out if "anyone" is thirsty, his invitation invites those who are deeply in need of the Spirit. This includes those who live within a barren land, far away from the Jerusalem temple, and in dire need for spiritual nourishment. These soon-to-be-satisfied ones are assured with a boundless supply of water, which the writer interprets in terms of the Spirit. For the Greek readers in the diaspora who hold no legitimate claim or access to the Jewish temple or the Jewish covenant promises, they now become the center of God's overflowing Spirit for simply having faith in Jesus. For Jesus, Jerusalem is not the center of God's overflowing water.

32. Joel 3:18; Zech 13:1; 14:8; Rev 22:1.
33. Isa 12:3; 49:10; 55:1; 58:11; Sir 24:30–31; 2 Bar. 77:13–16.

Jesus's statement transfers the fulfillment of the prophecy from the Jerusalem temple to those who believe in him. In a sense, anyone who approaches Jesus, including Greeks, becomes the sanctuary of God. No temple, including the one in Jerusalem, can contain the overflowing wells of the Spirit that will pour out upon all people who dwell in various geographical locations throughout the Roman Empire.

THE SPIRIT FLOWS UPON ALL FLESH

John 7 begins with Jesus being rejected in Galilee by his family and concludes with the religious leaders debating Jesus's identity in Jerusalem. Amid this hostile and escalating drama, another layer includes the suspicion that Jesus is going to reach out to the Greeks. Right after this charge of desiring to gain new disciples among the Greeks, Jesus invites anyone who believes in him to receive the Spirit. The invitation to receive the Spirit was sparked by the accusation that Jesus would dare to go to the Greeks in the diaspora. As we can observe above, Jesus's description of the Spirit draws upon various prophetic promises that anticipate the pouring of the Holy Spirit upon God's people. This kaleidoscope of multifarious images embraces the assumption that the Spirit will indiscriminately flow within people who dare to approach Jesus. While the water-Spirit imagery may allude to various scriptural themes, our reading includes another contextual dynamic: the recognition that the dialogue is ethnically hostile and that the true interpreters of Jesus's invitation include racially diverse readers—especially Greeks.

The promise of the Spirit is not only drawing from these prophetic hopes, but it is also transposed for a new audience that understands the struggles and challenges between Greeks and Jews. If anyone is spiritually thirsty or in a place where God feels distant or out of reach, Jesus's promise offers hope. He assures that the Spirit will become an overflowing well of water within them, bringing life to those spiritually dying of thirst. What is most remarkable about Jesus's invitation is the following. When Jesus undergoes suspicion and rejection from his own family and people, this does not prevent him from indiscriminately offering the Spirit to anyone who believes. This "anyone" really means just that—anyone living in any place and from any culture or racial background. No matter where a person is or how distant they feel from God, the waters of the Spirit can still reach their parched land.

6

The Family of God (John 13–16)

IN JOHN 13, WE come across a story of Jesus celebrating a Passover meal with his disciples. The disciples find themselves alone with Jesus, perhaps unaware that they will never again celebrate this meal with him. The words Jesus gives during these final days of his life are known as the Farewell Discourse within chs. 13–17 of John's Gospel. A farewell discourse is a literary genre that preserves the final words of a beloved figure before the person dies.[1] Raymond Brown describes these words in John's Gospel as "Jesus's last testament."[2] Farewell dialogues are found throughout biblical and Jewish literature.[3] Within the New Testament, a prominent farewell address is Paul's message to the elders of the Ephesian church

---

1. Sheridan, "Paraclete as Successor," 129–30; Segovia, *Farewell of the Word*, vii–viii; Stube, *Graeco-Roman Rhetorical Reading*, 81.

2. R. Brown, *Gospel According to John*, 2:582.

3. This includes Jacob's blessing of his children before his death (Gen 47:29—49:33), Joshua's speech to Israel (Josh 22–24), and David's final speech (1 Chr 28–29). In fact, the entire book of Deuteronomy is also considered as Moses's farewell address to the Hebrew people. Other patriarchal figures who give farewell addresses include Enoch, Noah, Abraham, Isaac, Rebecca, Ezra, and Baruch. See also 1 En. 91–108; Jub. 10:1–15; 20:1—23:1; 35:1—36:18; 4 Ezra 14:27–48; 2 Bar. 77–87; T. Dan 2:1; 5:7–8; T. Gad 4:1–7; T. Jos. 1:1; T. Levi 1:2; 4:1; 13:5–7; T. Naph. 1:2–5; 4:1–5; 9:2; T. Reu. 1:2–4; T. Sim. 1:2; 3:1–2; 5:1–5; T. Mos. 1:15.

The Family of God (John 13–16)

right before he is arrested in Jerusalem (Acts 20:17–38). However, there is something different with Jesus's teachings in John's Gospel, not found in any other Gospel. The Holy Spirit emerges in this discourse and is called the "Paraclete," often translated as "Comforter" or "Helper."[4] However, the portrayal of the Holy Spirit as the Comforter, Helper, or Paraclete within contemporary scholarship is often described solely in terms of coming to the disciples in order to reveal, testify, defend, or provide truth to the disciples.

Understanding the Paraclete in a forensic, testifying, and revelatory manner makes sense considering the way in which Jesus describes the activities of the Paraclete. For example, Jesus alerts the disciples that he will ask the Father for another Paraclete, also described as the "Spirit of Truth," who will be with the disciples forever (John 14:16–17). Additionally, the Paraclete is portrayed as the "Holy Spirit" who will teach and remind the disciples of Jesus's words (v. 26). Much later, Jesus makes mention that the Paraclete will provide a testimony of Jesus's identity. The disciples, who are promised to have the Paraclete, will also testify about Jesus's identity to the world. Testimony will occur in and through the disciples (15:26–27).[5] This eagerness for the Paraclete's presence is also expressed as an advantage for the disciples. Jesus recognizes that when the Paraclete comes, he will also convict the world of sin, righteousness, and judgment (16:7–15). Overall, the identity and mission of the Paraclete seems straightforward and uncomplicated, but something else is going on here, more than simply a description of the Paraclete as a revealer, teacher, or defender, which I want to focus on in this chapter.

Throughout all the various discussions on the Paraclete, what has not been considered is how the Spirit-Paraclete sayings also contribute to a reimagining of racial identity and family belonging. In fact, the presence of the Paraclete makes it possible for the

---

4. For example, the NRSV, NET, NLT, and NAB translate the term as "advocate." The NASB, NKJV, and ESV prefer "helper." The NIV and CSB translate παράκλητος as "counselor." The NJB prefers the transliteration "Paraclete" although the term is not an English word. For a definition see Estrada, *Pneumatology of Race*, 213–21.

5. See Estrada, "Spirit as Inner Witness."

disciples and readers of the Gospel to develop a new racialized identity as "children of God," an identity that shapes how they view themselves and others. But what is the relationship between the Spirit-Paraclete and racial identity and family belonging? Does the Spirit-Paraclete really have anything to say about racial or family relations? I believe so. This chapter provides compelling reasons why we must reconsider our understanding of the Paraclete's identity in light of familial language. Within the Farewell Discourse of John's Gospel, we cannot fail to notice that Jesus starts to call the disciples his children and begins to observe them as members of his own family. These are not merely terms of endearment. It aims to change how they understand themselves and relate to one another, including the Spirit.

As such, I examine how this family imagery within the Farewell Discourse and Gospel provides the appropriate lens to understand the Paraclete's identity and activity. Last, I incorporate these views in order to reimagine how the presence of the Spirit-Paraclete as an advocate, revealer, teacher, and ultimately, the Holy Spirit, creates a new understanding of family belonging for the disciples and Johannine community. My hope is that we cannot simply think of the Paraclete as an abstract spiritual presence that simply communicates knowledge or information. The Paraclete is the Spirit of God who gives a voice to the voiceless. The Paraclete remains present among the children of God who have no one else to defend or speak for them. Most importantly, the Paraclete demonstrates that the family of God is now present within the world. Without the Paraclete, we are utterly orphans with no family to call our own.

THE FAREWELL DISCOURSE AND ITS FAMILIAL LANGUAGE

Unquestionably, Jesus's final words are given to his disciples in the same manner that a father figure would give his final words to his own children. We cannot ignore how the farewell address, generally given to family members, must also shape how we are

The Family of God (John 13–16)

to understand notions of racial identity and belonging. But what is the evidence that there is a reimagining and forming of a new community? How do we know that the Paraclete should be interpreted in terms of a familial imagery? To put it simply, throughout the Farewell Discourse, Jesus refers to the disciples as children and admits that without the Paraclete, they would be like orphans. This new way of understanding his relationship with the disciples, as I argue, is the Gospel's way of reimagining one's sense of racial identity and family belonging.

It is important to recognize that when we talk about the notions of a child and an orphan, we are essentially discussing the family and its broader members. During this period, a person's identity was dependent and emerged from within the family—a family rooted at the center of a kinship and racial group. Since a family member is also a member of a larger kinship and racial community, any child born within a family is thus placed in relation not only with their immediate kin but with their historic ancestors, whose reputation also plays a formative role for the child. We thus can notice why there was such a heightened emphasis upon lineages in the ancient world and on ensuring that the proper children are born and belong to the family. Lineages establish family relations, identity, and group belonging, and link a child to an ancestor.

The relation between a child and his or her community is evident in Cicero's description of human relations. Cicero was a Roman statesman who identified the network of relations that a person has, starting with the universal bond of humanity to the more intimate close connection of a child. He states:

> Then, too, there are a great many degrees of closeness or remoteness in human society. To proceed beyond the universal bond of our common humanity, there is the closer one of belonging to the same people, tribe, and tongue, by which men are very closely bound together; it is a still closer relation to be citizens of the same city-state; for fellow-citizens have much in common. . . . But a still closer social union exists between kindred, starting with that infinite bond of union of the human race in general,

> the conception is now confined to a small and narrow circle. For since the reproductive instinct is by Nature's gift the common possession of all living creatures, the first bond of union is that between husband and wife; the next, that between parents and children; then we find one home, with everything in common. And this is the foundation of civil government, the nursery, as it were, of the state.[6]

One thing we must notice is how Cicero places much value on family bonds. In other words, at the most basic unit, the family is the strongest place of belonging, but Cicero does not end here. He also mentions that if a question is asked about the most important obligation, it would first be the state and then the family. He states:

> Country would come first, and parents; for their services have laid us under the heaviest obligation; next come children and the whole family, who look to us alone for support and can have no other protection; finally, our kinsmen, with whom we live on good terms and with whom, for the most part, our lot is one.[7]

Notice again, there is no such thing as a free individual apart from a larger network of people. An individual who is part of the family is a member of one community, whether a state, empire, or racial group.

Aristotle, writing much earlier than Cicero, puts it another way by explaining the relation between the individual and the larger community. Aristotle reflects a Greek perspective that valued the importance of the community over and against the interest of the individual. He, too, asserts:

> It is clear therefore that the state is also prior by nature to the individual; for if each individual when separate is not self-sufficient, he must be related to the whole state as other parts are to their whole, while a man who is incapable of entering into partnership, or who is so

---

6. Cicero, *On Duties* 1.53–1.54.
7. Cicero, *On Duties* 1.58.

self-sufficing that he has no need to do so, is no part of a state, so that he must be either a lower animal or a god.[8]

As we can notice in the above quote, there is no such thing as an isolated individual who exists apart from the larger community. Aristotle considers this part of the nature of the civic life and community.

Athenian Greeks such as Aristotle believed that no individual could exist without the state. Though Aristotle slightly differs from Cicero, the point thus remains—the family is an essential and important web of belonging, and all people are members of a larger community. Children are not only members of their family, but they are embedded within a larger network that includes their ancestors, racial communities, and the state. No child exists apart from a network of relations with people. To exist apart from others, as Aristotle concludes, is to be "a lower animal or a god."[9]

Turning back to Jesus's teaching about the Paraclete in John's Farewell Discourse, we notice that at the beginning of the conversation, Jesus is aware that his departure from the world is at hand and that he is going to return to the Father. This departure has grave consequences for the disciples. Jesus knows that he is going to leave the disciples. He washes their feet and predicts a betrayal, prompting Judas to depart from the group (13:2–30). Afterward, Jesus again states that the time for his "glorification" has come, which creates anticipation of Jesus's death (vv. 31–32).[10] After cryptically warning the disciples about his glorification, Jesus describes them as "little children" who will no longer experience his presence (v. 33). The disciples do not understand what this means. We find here for the first time the disciples being called "little children," which is not the first time this language is used to describe the believers in John's Gospel. We will get to this point later, but right now, Jesus continues to inform the disciples that they will not be able to find him, thus ensuring the reality of his departure. Peter

---

8. Aristotle, *Politics* 1253a.
9. Aristotle, *Politics* 1253a.
10. John 7:39; 12:16, 23.

responds to this news with the bold assertion that he will follow Jesus wherever he goes, but Peter does not know that he will soon deny Jesus (vv. 34–38).

This state of pending abandonment—not knowing where Jesus is going, what Jesus means about his moment of glorification, and the sudden realization that the disciples will no longer see Jesus—sets the tone for ch. 14 where the teaching on the Holy Spirit as a Paraclete begins. Jesus exhorts the disciples to not be troubled but to believe in the Father and in him (14:1). He again explains his departure and return in terms of going away to his "Father's house" to prepare a place for them (vv. 2–6). This description of going to his "Father's house" includes the declaration that if they know Jesus, then they know the Father and thus have already seen him (v. 7). At this point, Philip asks Jesus to reveal the Father. Jesus replies, "He who has seen me has seen the Father" (v. 9) and claims, "I am in the Father and the Father is in Me" (v. 11). The unity and distinction between the Father and Jesus are emphasized in this response to Philip and the disciples. In fact, mention of the "Father" is found twenty-three times within this chapter alone. In these passages, as William Loader suggests, Jesus stands for the Father in the world and allows the Father to work and speak through him.[11] Or, as Bultmann also states, Jesus redirects the attention of the disciples to the indirect vision of God in himself.[12] Throughout this Farewell Discourse, the relationships between Jesus, the disciples, and God are being reimagined. Even more, since John 13:33, the disciples are also described as "little children" about to experience the most drastic event that can happen to a child: becoming orphaned. Although Jesus is not the Father, the Farewell Discourse is woven with family imagery that portrays Jesus as a father who speaks to his children, warning them about his coming death and the responsibilities thereafter.

Now, some remark that by calling the disciples "children" in 13:33, this is simply affectionate language.[13] Perhaps, but this

---

11. Loader, *Jesus in John's Gospel*, 345.
12. Bultmann, *Gospel of John*, 608.
13. Stube, *Graeco-Roman Rhetorical Reading*, 98.

The Family of God (John 13–16)

language is not a new metaphor for believers or the Johannine community. Since the Prologue in 1:12, those who believe in Jesus are given the right to be a "child of God." The Prologue foreshadows major theological themes that will be developed within the narrative. By stating that those who believe will be authorized to be God's children, the text emphatically pronounces that Jesus holds the singular power to determine who is a member of the family of God. The Prologue rejects the limitations that lineages have in the construction and maintenance of racial identity, relations, and inheritance. It rejects the assumption that one is a child of God due solely to birthing and ancestry relations (v. 13).[14] As argued in the previous chapters, these are also themes and issues related to the role and activity of the Spirit within John's Gospel.

Since the Prologue of John's Gospel, the Gospel writer has attempted to compel us to understand the notion of a new family based on the presence and activity of the Spirit. In other words, the phrase "children of God" in the Prologue, the Spirit's begetting of those who believe in Jesus, and the "little children" in the Farewell Discourse are linked together through and as a result of the Spirit-Paraclete who gives birth to the people of God. Even more, in John 11:52, the Gospel writer explains that the death of Jesus will gather all the "children" of God scattered throughout the diaspora. Though the mention of the children of God is a reflection on Caiaphas's statement to the Jewish religious leaders, the Gospel writer interprets these words as an unintended prophecy about the impact of Jesus's death for all people who believe (v. 52).

The Gospel readers know what it means to be a child of God. When we turn to the Johannine Letters, the recipients of John's letters are called "children of God" because they have been granted this new identity through their faith in Jesus and birth in the Spirit.[15] This new identity within the family of God is language that enables the readers to reimagine what it means to belong to God and each other. Just as the Greeks and Romans distinguished

---

14. Estrada, *Latino Reading of Race*, 111–41.
15. 1 John 2:1, 12, 28; 3:1–2, 7, 10, 18; 4:4; 5:2, 21; 2 John 1:1, 4, 13; 3 John 1:4.

themselves from the barbarians and the Jews distinguished themselves from the gentiles, so too are the readers of John's Gospel being made to reimagine and expand the boundaries of racial belonging and members of God's household. Since Jesus promises to send the Paraclete to the disciples, this should dispel all notions of abandonment or rejection. The presence and activity of the Paraclete within and among the disciples demonstrates that the believers are God's children. As Jesus states, "I will not leave you orphaned, I will come to you" (14:18). Undeniably, without the Spirit-Paraclete, the disciples would indeed be orphans—lost and ostracized from their own kin and racial community.

ORPHANS IN ANTIQUITY

Now, this orphan imagery is not accidental. As noted in the previous section, the family was vital for the construction of one's identity and sense of belonging in the ancient world. The orphan description, inversely, is the language of exclusion. The status of orphans was an unfortunate reality in the ancient world. Although today we identify orphans with those who have lost both parents, this was not always so. In the Greek and Roman patriarchal culture, it referred to someone who had solely lost one's father. Only later in the sixth century (CE) did the term refer to a child who had lost both parents.[16] The Gospel's use of this vivid reality not only refers to the most vulnerable and defenseless in Greco-Roman world, but it also portrays how many would have viewed the disciples and the Johannine community after Jesus's death and departure. Consequently, I want to briefly elaborate in this section the status of orphans in Greek and biblical literature to deepen our understanding of the Gospel's usage of this term in the Farewell Discourse. As I will emphasize, the presence of the Spirit-Paraclete upon and within the disciples confirms the presence and emergence of the new family of God.

---

16. Fitzgerald, "Orphans in Mediterranean Antiquity," 30.

The Family of God (John 13–16)

First, to think about orphans is to come to terms with the reality of a father's death. Sabine Hübner points out that ancient fatherlessness was rooted in this pervasive and endemic reality. Hübner finds that there were many fatherless children, given the high mortality rate of men and their tendency to marry late in life.[17] Walter Scheidel notices that about one-third of all children would have lost their father by the age of fifteen.[18] J. T. Fitzgerald points to further conditions that would have contributed to early paternal death such as disease, short life expectancy, and war.[19] Overall, a father's death put a child's inheritance at risk, gave undue hardship and grief to the mother, and created the possibility of becoming susceptible to oppression and exploitation.[20] The situation was even worse for orphaned girls, who would have difficulties raising the required dowry for marriage.[21] These were some of the most difficult situations that would befall all orphans, regardless of social status.

These challenges certainly motivated many widows to immediately remarry, but this did not always solve the problem. Hübner finds that in Roman law, the stepfathers were depicted as legacy hunters who aimed to embezzle their stepchildren's inheritance.[22] They actively sought out widows to take advantage of their situation and gain immediate wealth. Although guardians were appointed to safeguard the inheritance of orphans, the laws applied only to Roman citizens.[23] This left most non-Roman orphans without legal protection. Even more, orphans were at the mercy of stepfathers, who were not legally obligated to provide for them.[24] Certainly, the widow was now taken care of through remarriage. The situation of an orphan was not guaranteed to become

17. Hübner, "Fatherless Antiquity," 9.
18. Scheidel, "Demographic Background."
19. Fitzgerald, "Orphans in Mediterranean Antiquity," 30–34.
20. Hübner, "Fatherless Antiquity," 10–13.
21. Hübner, "Fatherless Antiquity," 11.
22. Hübner, "Callirhoe's Dilemma," 64–67.
23. Hübner, "Callirhoe's Dilemma," 67.
24. Hübner, "Callirhoe's Dilemma," 81.

ameliorated with the intervention of a stepfather, guardian, older siblings, or extended kin. The harsh consequences of being orphaned were difficult to alleviate.

A notable example is found in the Homeric epics. When Hector of Troy died after his fight with Achilles, his wife Andromache was not immediately aware of the situation. She assumed that Hector was going to defeat Achilles. But when she hears cries from the hallways, she runs to the walls of Troy only to find her husband's body dragged through the dirt. She bursts into tears at the realization of Hector's death. In her lament, the impact that his death would have on their son emerges, and she states,

> You leave [me] in chilling grief, a widow in your halls, and your son is still a mere babe, the son born of you and me, both ill-fated; nor will you be any profit to him, Hector, since you are dead, nor he to you. For even though he escapes the woeful war of the Achaeans, yet will his portion be labor and sorrow afterwards, for others will take away his lands. The day of orphanhood cuts a child off from the friends of his youth; ever is his head bowed low, and his cheeks are bathed in tears, and in his need the child goes up to his father's friends, plucking one by the cloak and another by the tunic; and of them that are touched with pity, one holds out his cup for a moment: his lips he wets, but his palate he wets not. And one whose father and mother still live thrusts him from the feast striking him with his hand, and reproaches him with reviling words: "Off with you, quick! No father of yours feasts in our company." Then in tears to his widowed mother comes back the child—Astyanax, who once on his father's knees ate only marrow and the rich fat of sheep; and when sleep came on him and he ceased from his childish play, then would he slumber in a bed in the arms of his nurse, in his soft bed, his heart filled with good things. But now, since he has lost his dear father, he will suffer many ills.[25]

---

25. Homer, *Iliad* 22.484–22.500.

The Family of God (John 13–16)

The dire fate of Hector's son is not lost in Andromache's words. She realizes that Astyanax's life has drastically changed because of Hector's death. Astyanax, a child who was once eating in luxury, will be cast out from the table, beaten by strangers, having no one to protect him, ridiculed, deprived of his land, and socially ostracized from his friends. From a life of luxury, Astyanax, the orphaned son, will now have a life of labor and "suffer many ills." If Andromache's speech reveals a situation that could happen to the powerful, how much more dire a situation for orphans who do not have access to the privileges of royalty? The death of a father places a child's economic, social, and inheritance in jeopardy.

Although not all orphans were neglected, all of them—both the wealthy and poor—faced economic and social challenges. Though Zeus was known to be a god who watched over orphans in Greek mythology,[26] a similar portrait emerges in biblical literature. Similar to Greek literature, a central characteristic of orphans in the Old Testament is the lack of rights and their defenseless position in society.[27] This is notable in the various injunctions to care for and protect orphans, especially since they are most susceptible to being oppressed, murdered, sold as slaves; experiencing theft and financial distress; and being denied justice.[28] Due to these harsh experiences, God emerges as their surrogate father and protector. God promises to hear the cries of orphans and avenge them (Exod 22:22–27). God is also portrayed as executing justice for orphans (Deut 10:18). The psalmist also considers God as a "helper of the orphan ... who inclines his ear to vindicate the orphan and oppressed" (Ps 10:14, 17–18). Or as more poignantly described, "He is a father to the fatherless" (68:5). And in Hosea the prophet claims, "For in you the orphan finds mercy" (14:3). God in the Old Testament is deeply concerned about the status and welfare of orphans and is depicted as their defender. As a result, the Israelite

---

26. Hesiod, *Op.* 327–34.
27. Sigismund, "'Without Father,'" 87.
28. Exod 22:22; Deut 10:18; 14:28–29; 24:17–22; 26:12–13; 27:19; 2 Kgs 4:1; Job 24:9; 29:12; 31:17–22; Ps 94:6; Prov 23:10; Isa 1:17, 23; Jer 5:28; 7:6; 22:3; Ezek 22:7; Zech 7:10; Mal 3:5.

community is given an injunction to protect and provide for them, not causing them any more undue hardship. Although the New Testament rarely mentions orphans, the same command to care for orphans is assumed. In particular, Jesus demonstrates his ability to raise a dead orphan boy who was the only son of a widow in a town called Nain. This miracle led many to affirm that God had come to help his people, thus truly caring for orphans (Luke 7:11–16). James describes true religion as "caring for the orphans and widows in their misfortune" (Jas 1:27).

In light of the above exploration, it is fairly reasonable to conclude that orphans were truly the most vulnerable in antiquity. The threat of social and economic instability caused by losing one's father was a problem for children. Being orphaned left children defenseless and vulnerable to oppression and exploitation, thus in need not only of their family but also of an advocate. It is not a coincidence that children today, those who experience maltreatment and abuse, including those in the foster care system, also experience poorer communication development and have social communication delays and a limited vocabulary.[29] Without advocacy, orphans would be in an utterly disastrous situation. They need somebody to defend them and help them gain their voice. Perhaps this is why the Spirit-Paraclete testifies not only to the world but also through and to the disciples. As we can notice in the above letter, not all orphans and widows were immediately taken care of by their extended kin. In fact, there were no orphanages during antiquity until the mid-fourth century.[30]

THE FAMILY OF GOD AND THE SPIRIT-PARACLETE

Turning back to John's Gospel, what can we conclude? How do the familial language and reality of being orphaned in the ancient world impact our understanding of the Paraclete's identity and

---

29. Hwa-Froelich, *Social Communication Development*, 273–303.
30. Fitzgerald, "Orphans in Mediterranean Antiquity," 44.

The Family of God (John 13–16)

activity? My hope is that we can realize that the forensic terminology to describe the Spirit does not emerge by accident in John's Gospel. The sending of the Spirit as Paraclete therefore compels us to bring to the forefront of our imagination the role of advocacy for the fatherless, including the newly born children of God who are also known as the disciples and Johannine community. The distressing experiences of being a believer, the fear of abandonment by one's family, synagogue expulsion, and rejection from one's own racial community for simply confessing faith in Jesus is mitigated by the sending of the Spirit-Paraclete. Jesus's promise to send the Spirit-Paraclete communicates a hope for the children of God—those orphaned, abandoned, excommunicated, on the verge of poverty, with their land and inheritance in jeopardy, but nonetheless born of the Spirit. If anyone needs a defender in the ancient world, it is children, as the voiceless and the most vulnerable of society who need an advocate more than anyone else. This advocate is the Spirit of God—the Paraclete.[31]

For the readers of the Gospel, they would be forever spiritually orphaned and without rights, privileges, and access to the family of God without the Paraclete. Since they truly have the Paraclete with them, however, the believers who have diverse families and racial identities are held together and secure as God's newly born children—those no longer bound to racial and family relations. As such, this portrayal of the Spirit as Paraclete provides the opportunity for the disciples to view themselves as a newly formed family of God joined and united to one another. All notions of racial identity and family relations are reimagined and reconstructed as a result of the Spirit-Paraclete's presence.

With this in mind, we can now understand the revelatory and forensic benefits of the Paraclete. Believers are no longer alone. They belong to the family of God. As members of this family, they receive assurance that the Spirit of God, the Paraclete, will come to them, be within them, and defend them. This includes remembering and relearning the teachings of Jesus (14:26), experiencing the testifying activity of the Paraclete and Spirit of Truth

---

31. For a contextual reading, see Estrada, "What Does the Paraclete."

(15:26–27), and participating in the convicting power of the Paraclete (16:7–15). The Spirit-Paraclete will neither leave the disciples as victims nor be absent or passive, for Jesus promises a judicial response. This activity of the Spirit-Paraclete occurs not just in the conscience of the disciples or before the courtroom of God but in the proclamation of the community. It is made manifest through resistance to oppression and injustice. The Spirit-Paraclete is active throughout the world as a prosecuting attorney in all spaces, preparing a case against the oppressive rulers and people who take advantage of God's children.

7

Harnessing Courage Through the Spirit (John 20)

AT THE CONCLUSION OF John's Gospel, Jesus manifests himself to only ten disciples locked in a room because they are afraid of the Jews (John 20:19–23). Jesus's presence provides the opportunity to demonstrate his resurrected body (v. 20). This appearance leads the disciples to rejoice because they have seen the Lord. Right after this appearance, Jesus commissions the disciples with a similar charge that he received from the Father (v. 21). At this moment he breathes upon them the Holy Spirit and explains their role in the forgiveness of sins. The giving of the Spirit in this resurrection scene presents a perspective that differs from Acts and the commission scenes of the Synoptic Gospels. In John's Gospel, the disciples are not instructed to wait for the Spirit as we find in Acts 1:8. Instead, Jesus breathes upon them with the exhortation to receive the Holy Spirit. Furthermore, in John's Gospel the disciples are in a locked room because they are afraid of the Jews. The setting of John 20:19–23 is a context of fear, whereas the Synoptics describe fear occurring only at the tomb.[1] Considering this, how are we to understand the giving of the Holy Spirit in light of this "fear of the Jews"? Is John's Gospel attempting to reinterpret Jesus's

---

1. Matt 28:8, 10; Mark 16:8.

commission in light of their fear? Furthermore, is this a commission to reach those who participated in or condoned the synagogue excommunication, hatred, and death of their fellow members?

In this last discussion about the Spirit in John's Gospel, I propose that we ought to understand the giving of the Holy Spirit in John 20:22 not just as a desire to empower the disciples for mission or to grant them the authorization to forgive sins. What is missing from our interpretation of this episode is how the giving of the Spirit is done within the context of empowering the disciples with a fearless ability to cross boundaries—that is, to reach the world, those beyond the social, cultural, and racial boundaries of one's own homogenous people. This also means that the disciples and readers of the Gospel cannot authentically imitate the Father's sending of the Son as Spirit breathed upon individuals if they continue to have a fear of the other, or in this case, a fear of "the Jews."

How do we know that this boundary-crossing reading is the most appropriate for the giving of the Holy Spirit? Primarily, we must notice the way in which fear permeates John's description of Jesus's appearances to the disciples. Second, we also must notice that the context of fear, that is, a "fear of the Jews," does not really make much sense unless this also applies to the readers. When we take these elements together, we can understand a more robust understanding of the Holy Spirit who empowers us to navigate and bridge cultural and racial divides. My hope, again, with this chapter and others, is that we can notice how the Holy Spirit in John's Gospel is very much concerned with helping the readers move beyond their fear of the other and boldly preach the gospel wherever the Spirit may send them.

JOHN'S RESURRECTION APPEARANCE AND THE SYNOPTIC GOSPELS

From Jesus's resurrection appearance to the giving of the Holy Spirit, John's Gospel is strikingly different than the Synoptic Gospels. John's resurrection story begins with Mary Magdalene, who, for some reason unexplained, goes to the tomb early in the morning

Harnessing Courage Through the Spirit (John 20)

(John 20:1). Slightly after Mary Magdalene notices the empty tomb, she reports to the disciples that Jesus's body was taken (v. 2). When Peter and the beloved disciple see for themselves that the tomb is indeed empty, we can understand why they leave and say nothing. They perhaps believed that Jesus's body was desecrated by bandits. Although the Gospel explains that only the beloved disciple "believed," we are unsure whether he really understood the resurrection implications of the empty tomb (vv. 8–10). However, they both leave Mary Magdalene weeping alone outside the tomb (v. 11). While she is alone, two angels appear and ask why she weeps (v. 13). Then she encounters another person, whom she misidentifies as the gardener, and hears the same question (v. 15). After hearing the gardener call her by name, she recognizes that Jesus is speaking to her. She attempts to cling onto him, but Jesus commands her to tell the disciples that he is going to ascend to the Father (v. 17). Mary Magdalene immediately leaves to inform the disciples that she has "seen the Lord" and spoken to him (v. 18).

Knowledge of Jesus's resurrection did not seem to have an immediate impact on the disciples. Instead, they are described as gathered behind locked doors "in fear of the Jews" (v. 19). This state of fear seems bizarre, given that they had previously received a report from Mary Magdalene that Jesus had appeared. Is it possible that they, as the noncanonical Gospel of Peter suggests, were afraid of the Jews because of false rumors that were being spread about them?[2] Regardless, according to John's Gospel, in this state of fear, Jesus appears, saying on two occasions "peace be with you" (vv. 19, 21). Jesus demonstrates his hands and side, which leads the disciples to be overwhelmed with joy (v. 20). Jesus then tells them, "As the Father has sent me, I also send you." While saying these words he breathes upon them and continues, "Receive the Holy Spirit." This call to receive the Holy Spirit comes with the pronouncement that the disciples would have authority to forgive and retain sins. But did they respond and receive? There is no reaction from the disciples as we are accustomed to observing in

---

2. See Gos. Pet. 7–15.

other passages within the New Testament.³ Instead, we are made aware that this appearance was for only ten disciples. Thomas was absent from the group, and it takes an entire week before he gets the chance to see Jesus for himself (vv. 24–29). Yet, the fear still lingers. The disciples still gather behind locked doors even though they have seen the Lord and know that he is alive (v. 26). Why such fear? Why keep locking the doors and remaining in a state of fear of "the Jews"?

In this brief review, we can observe that the Johannine resurrection episode departs from the Synoptics in a variety of ways. The story of Mary Magdalene conversing alone with Jesus is found only in John's Gospel. In the Synoptics a variety of women come to the tomb, but they do not have a comparable dialogue as we find in John's Gospel.⁴ The differences are striking when we try to identify the divine figures who also appear at the tomb. None of the Gospels agree on who or how many divine figures appeared.⁵ It is difficult not only to find parallels between all the Gospels but also to identify their literary relationship. What we can affirm is that many stories in John's Gospel are unique, including this story of Jesus appearing to Mary Magdalene and then to the ten disciples who were gathered together behind locked doors (20:1–23).

The differences should not be understood as to presume that John's Gospel is the only Gospel that departs from some core tradition. Many resurrection stories in the Gospel tradition are unique to each writer.⁶ What do all these distinct traditions suggest? Does this propose that the resurrection stories are unreliable? Scholars do recognize the problems that John's Gospel has with any

---

3. Similar exhortations to "receive the Spirit" include physical manifestations, reactions, or responses to the characters in Acts 1:8; 2:38; 8:15, 17, 19; 10:47; 19:2.

4. Compare Matt 28:1–2, 9–10; Mark 16:1–3; Luke 24:1–2.

5. Compare Matt 28:2; Mark 16:5; Luke 24:4–5; John 20:12.

6. For example, the stories of the guards at the tomb (Matt 28:11–15); Jesus appearing on the road to Emmaus (Mark 16:12–13; Luke 24:13–45); the ascension accounts (Mark 16:15–19; Luke 24:44–53); Jesus appearing to over five hundred people (1 Cor 15:3–8); and various appearances throughout forty days (Acts 1:3).

historical tradition.[7] Regardless of the difficulties that the various resurrection stories present, this may also suggest that John's Gospel represents a perspective that is no more authentic or inauthentic than others. John's Gospel has a retelling of Jesus's final days that is unique and distinct for its own context and circumstance. What, then, is the context and circumstance of the Gospel's exhortation to receive the Spirit in John 20:22? Quite simply, it is the fear of the "other." We can see this more acutely when we compare the giving of the Spirit in John's Gospel to the Synoptics and Acts. Fear is what makes John's retelling of the story distinct.

The earliest version of Mark do not include Jesus's final words, which suggests that there was no commission.[8] It is only in the longer ending of Mark 16:14–20 where Jesus appears to the disciples while they are sitting at a table. He commissions them to go into the world and preach the gospel to all creation. This Markan mission to all creation is promised to be accompanied with signs, which include the ability to cast out demons, speak in tongues, become unaffected by serpents and poisonous drinks, and heal the sick (vv. 17–18). There is a presumption that their mission will include manifestations of divine power, but the Spirit is not mentioned. Luke presents the commission occurring in Jerusalem when the disciples were gathered together (Luke 24:44–53). Jesus appears in order to "open their minds to understand Scripture" (v. 45). He explains the significance of his death and resurrection from the Law and the Prophets, and that the message of repentance and forgiveness of sins should be preached in all nations. Jesus urges them to also wait for the Spirit, who will "clothe them with power from on high" (v. 49). Then he walks out to Bethany, blesses the disciples, and ascends to heaven (vv. 50–51). In Luke's Gospel, Jesus is involved in explaining Scripture and promises to give the Holy Spirit at a later time. According to Matthew, the disciples are already on a mountain in Galilee where they meet Jesus

---

7. Ashton, *Understanding the Fourth Gospel*, 486; Blomberg, *Historical Reliability*, 259; Sanders, *Historical Figure of Jesus*, 278–80; Moloney, *Resurrection of the Messiah*, 139–47; Allison, *Resurrecting Jesus*, 269.

8. Metzger, *Textual Commentary*, 102–6.

The Spirit in John's Gospel

(Matt 28:16–20). Some disciples respond to Jesus's appearance by worshiping him, while others still doubt (v. 17). Jesus then states that he has all authority in heaven and earth and that they should make disciples of all nations, baptizing them and teaching them all that he commanded (vv. 18–19). In Matthew's account, the Spirit is mentioned only in the formula for early Christian baptism. There is no impartation or expectation that the Spirit will empower them in their mission to preach the gospel to all nations.

Given this, what are the implications for our understanding of the Spirit and his relationship to Jesus's giving of the Spirit in John's Gospel? Does this suggest that the giving of the Spirit in John's Gospel is a unique tradition? If anything, the diversity of the Gospel stories reveals that no Gospel writer has a more authentic preservation of Jesus's giving of the Spirit. Gary Burge, however, argues that John's Gospel records the full giving of the Spirit-Paraclete, which corresponds with Luke's account in Acts 2.[9] Though he highlights seven reasons why this is so, at the end of his analysis, he seems to cast doubt on his findings.[10] He claims that John's Gospel "has developed a traditional resurrection scene into a singular event uniting the return, the ascension, and the Spirit."[11] Though Burge attempts to make a case for viewing the giving of the Spirit in John 20:22 as a revision of Acts 2, others are not so generous.[12]

What then should we suppose? If anything, instead of attempting to find a literary relationship or influence between the Gospels, perhaps the best approach is to recognize that John's Gospel has its own resurrection tradition and does not find it necessary to draw from other Gospels because of the challenges his readers were facing at the end of the late first century. What is the probable reason that would motivate this unique portrayal of the Spirit in this commission scene? As this chapter will continue to

---

9. Burge, *Anointed Community*, 123.

10. Burge, *Anointed Community*, 125–30, 148.

11. Burge, *Anointed Community*, 131.

12. Barrett, *St. John*, 475; Porsch, *Pneuma und Wort*, 377–78; Turner, *Holy Spirit*, 92–99; Morris, *Gospel According to John*, 247–48.

argue, it was the fear of the "other." In other words, the giving of the Spirit was not solely an empowerment for mission. The added details about the "fear of the Jews" and setting of "locked doors" reveal that the writer of John's Gospel was keenly aware of the need for the disciples to overcome their fear of the other.

BREATHING THE SPIRIT AND THE "FEAR OF THE JEWS"

When we turn to the giving of the Spirit in John 20:22, many scholars rightly notice the link between the "breathing" of the Spirit upon the disciples and God's "breathing" upon Adam at creation in Gen 2:7.[13] The Greek term used to describe the act of "breathing" is found in both the Gospel of John and in Genesis. It is difficult to avoid noticing the allusion to the creation account in Genesis. Even more, this same term is also used to describe Ezekiel's vision to "breathe" on the valley of dry bones (Ezek 37:9). Shortly after Ezekiel obeys and the bones form into living beings, the Lord states, "I will put my Spirit within you, and you will come to life" (v. 14). The Spirit, nonetheless, gives life to the valley of dry bones and gives life to the first human being—Adam. The image of Jesus breathing the Holy Spirit on the disciples echoes the creation themes in Genesis and Ezekiel, inviting us to see Jesus as the one who, like God, breathes life into whom he wills. In fact, the Gospel has already been hinting at Jesus's ability to dispense the Spirit. Earlier in the Gospel, Jesus has promised to baptize people in the Holy Spirit (John 1:33) and to give the Spirit without measure (3:34). Thus, when Jesus breathes upon the disciples and invites them to receive the Spirit, this breath of life not only signifies a new creation, but it is also a breath of life that will help them move beyond their fear of the other—those who have engaged them with harm, threatened them, or even persecuted them.

---

13. Barrett, *St. John*, 474; Lindars, *Gospel of John*, 612; Keener, *Gospel of John*, 1204–5; R. Brown, *Gospel According to John*, 2:1035–37; Thompson, *John*, 421.

The Spirit in John's Gospel

Immediately after breathing upon the disciples, Jesus tells them that if they forgive the sins of anyone, their sins will be forgiven. If they do not, then their sins will remain (20:23). Now, how can they forgive sins if they have not encountered the other? How can they become a channel of God's mercy and grace if they are still locked behind closed doors and refuse to move beyond their own fear, prejudice, distrust, and sense of self-preservation? Fear is what is holding the disciples back, and it is fear keeping the doors locked to the wider world. Yet the context of fear is often a significant detail overlooked when interpreting the giving of the Spirit. For example, Bultmann suggests that the "fear of the Jews" is mentioned to emphasize the miraculous appearance of Jesus's arrival.[14] Samuel Pérez Millos speculates possible reasons why the disciples were gathered in fear, concluding that this "fear of the Jews" is really a fear of the religious leaders.[15] Of course, the question arises, who are the Jews? But perhaps the question we should really focus is the following: Who are the Jews to the readers of the Gospel?

From the context of a multiracial community in the late first century, this may refer to the Jewish religious authority.[16] But the mention of the "Jews" throughout the Gospel reflects the reality of a struggle between anti-Jewish and pro-Jewish attitudes within the John's community. The community itself is also constructing its identity in contrast to "the Jews" and "the world" as children of God. At this point in the narrative, John's community has now come to see itself as created and formed into a new lineage through the Spirit. We therefore must hear within this "fear of the Jews" the reflection of the community's experience with the racially other, including one's own kin who had abandoned and excommunicated them from the synagogue.

One may wonder why the narrator decided to include this emotional detail of fear. No other Gospel records the disciples' "fear of the Jews" or any other racial group, especially since the

---

14. Bultmann, *Gospel of John*, 690–91; Lindars, *Gospel of John*, 609–10.
15. Millos, *Juan*, 1772.
16. Keener, *Gospel of John*, 1200–201.

Romans had just executed Jesus.[17] Tricia Brown suggest that this fear reveals a sense of hiddenness and shame. She points out that people in Mediterranean societies are expected to have open doors. Since the doors in this scene are locked, this means that the disciples understood their behavior to be dishonorable, and thus the secrecy.[18] Keener suggests that mentioning the locked doors (vv. 21, 26) underlies the fear of the disciples, which is in contrast to the boldness implied for their mission to the world.[19] One can understand why the disciples were in fear. Their Messiah had just been betrayed, arrested in front of them, and executed by the Romans. They might have wondered if this same outcome of death was going to happen to them, but we know that no one was pursuing them. They were not even arrested with Jesus when the Romans apprehended him. Why then is there a "fear of the Jews" as if "the Jews" were still pursuing the disciples or attempting to arrest them? This statement, however, makes sense only when we think about the overall theme of "fear of the Jews" within the Gospel itself.

The phrase "fear of the Jews" first appears in John 7 during a Jewish festival. During this festival, some people from the crowds seek to apprehend and kill Jesus. They are looking for Jesus, and a debate emerges over his true identity. Some publicly defend Jesus's identity by saying that he is a good man, but when resistance to this positive proclamation of his identity emerges, it leads some to become silent. No one wants to defend Jesus against the charge that he is leading the people astray. No one desires to openly speak about him for "fear of the Jews" (7:13).

Who were these Jews? Of course, they would be people who are no different than those debating Jesus's identity and celebrating the Jewish festival. But from the vantage point of the reader, they

---

17. For example, Luke does record the disciples' fear. However, it is the result of seeing Jesus appear to them, not because they were afraid of the Jews or other ethnic group (Luke 24:36). Mark records the disciples having unbelief when Jesus appears (Mark 16:14). Matthew notices that some disciples worshiped Jesus while others had doubt (Matt 28:17).

18. T. Brown, *Spirit in Writings of John*, 106–7.

19. Keener, *Gospel of John*, 1201.

know that these are racially different people who hold the potential for resisting the claims of Jesus's true identity. Fear of the Jews in this context is a fear to publicly defend Jesus's identity among his own people. It is a fear that keeps one's mouth shut.

In 9:22, this "fear of the Jews" emerges again. In this context, it is a fear of the Jewish religious leaders who condoned and participated in eradicating members from the synagogue. In John 9, Jesus has recently healed a man who was born blind. The Jewish religious leaders interrogate the man and attempt to find out who had healed him. The blind man knows it was Jesus, and he calls him a prophet (9:17). The Jewish leaders do not believe in the man's confession and seek his parents. When the religious leaders find the parents, they equivocate and fail to confess that Jesus has healed their son. Instead, they tell the religious leaders to go consult their son and ask him. In other words, when they have the opportunity to testify of Jesus's miraculous power before the Jewish religious authorities, they balk. They do not speak the truth because they are "afraid of the Jews," given that these same religious leaders were involved in the synagogue expulsions. Fear keeps them from proclaiming Jesus's miraculous power and agreeing with their son that Jesus is indeed a prophet sent from God.

Last, in 19:38 we find a secret disciple named Joseph of Arimathea who approaches Pilate to ask for Jesus's body. He is a disciple of Jesus but one who follows from the distance. Nowhere in John's Gospel is Joseph mentioned, although he appears in the Synoptics as a member of the Jewish Council who sympathized with Jesus's message.[20] Perhaps he had come to know about Jesus just like Nicodemus but would not approach or interact with Jesus in public. Joseph nonetheless comes to Pilate in order to bury Jesus's body. This move may appear respectful and an attempt to give proper honor to Jesus's body, but one must also keep in mind that it is the failure to defend the oppressed that leads to dead bodies. Joseph would not openly associate himself with Jesus or defend his identity before those who maligned him because he, too, "feared the Jews." What does fear do in this context? Fear keeps him from

20. Matt 27:57; Mark 15:43; Luke 23:50–51.

publicly associating himself with Jesus. Fear keeps him away from defending Jesus's identity before those who falsely accuse him. Most disturbingly, fear allows him to stand by as violence befalls the innocent.

Why were the characters in John's Gospel so afraid? What did they fear so much that it led them to be silent amid resistance, false news about Jesus's identity, and violence against the innocent? Why did this fear paralyze them from speaking the truth and defending the innocent? We are unsure. We can notice, though, that the invitation to receive the Spirit is, in sum, an invitation to be infused with the divine creative and life-giving power of God's breath. Only with the Spirit can the disciples overcome their paralyzing fear of what can happen at the hands of the other.

Jesus summons the disciples to "receive the Holy Spirit," but did they receive the Spirit? There is no immediate response or reaction to the exhortation to receive the Spirit—no "speaking in tongues" or narrative affirmation that the disciples had indeed received the Spirit. We know that a week later they are still afraid and continuing to meet behind locked doors (20:26). Nonetheless, according to Jesus's words, we know that the disciples and readers of the Gospel needed to be infused with the Holy Spirit, who will propel them into the world and continue Jesus's mission on earth.

Said differently, John's Gospel understands the mission of the disciples as one infused by the Spirit and focused on reaching even those who cause much fear and have the power to do harm. The breathing of the Holy Spirit upon the disciples may be understood as a form of empowerment of divine life to reach those who threaten human life. The disciples need the Spirit to continue the mission. For this reason, Jesus prefaces the giving of the Spirit by saying, "Just as the Father has sent me, I send you all" (20:21).

BREATHING IN THE SPIRIT

How does one overcome the fear of the other in a racially hostile and xenophobic world? How does one faithfully execute Jesus's commission if one still holds onto a fear of "the Jews" or any other ethnic group? From John's perspective, the fear of the other is overcome by the Holy Spirit. John's Gospel presents its own Pentecost tradition by including the role of the Spirit in helping the disciples overcome their fear of "the Jews," which in the reader's context also includes the racially other. The Spirit infuses the disciples with the divine life-giving power to proclaim the message of Jesus's identity and reach those who participate or condone synagogue excommunication or who enact violence against the innocent. The life-giving Spirit is provided for the disciples and readers so they may no longer have a fear of what may happen if they interact or engage with the other.

Fear is paralyzing. It can grip the soul and prevent one from moving, speaking, and living a full life in the Spirit. Fear is often the symptom of an underlying trauma and overestimation of a particular threat.[21] Perhaps the disciples also had the fear of being rejected, expelled, or ridiculed for believing that Jesus was indeed the Messiah and Son of God. They might have had a fear of experiencing the same kind of violence that Jesus experienced on the cross. These are all fears that could inhibit the disciples and readers of the Gospel from continuing the mission of proclaiming Jesus's name. These fears could create the desire to disengage from the world and remain silent in a Roman and Greek polytheistic context.

Although John 20 begins with the disciples in a state of fear and within a locked room, in reality, these "Jews" they feared were the very people to whom Jesus came to grant eternal life. The disciples must breathe in the divine Spirit to be created anew. However, the Gospel does not specifically detail whether they received the Spirit. Did the disciples inhale the divine breath of life? The Gospel story does not provide an affirmative answer to this question. We know this answer only from the Lukan Pentecost of Acts 2. The ambiguity of this episode, nevertheless, provides an opportunity, for us—as the readers of the Gospel—to receive the divine Spirit and begin the work and mission in the world. Just like Jesus who became flesh and was sent into the world by the Father, this also

---

21. Abramowitz and Blakey, "Overestimation of Threat."

Harnessing Courage Through the Spirit (John 20)

means that he is commissioning us to inhabit the spaces of the racially other. We must continue this mission and proclaim the gospel of Jesus to all those we encounter. We must go outside of our own racial-cultural group and enter the world of the "other."

I know this may feel scary and push us outside of our comfort zones. The Gospel of John, nevertheless, concludes with a promise that the Spirit of God will give us the courage to enter into the world and engage the other. We can put aside our fears and breathe in the Holy Spirit as we journey into the world of the unknown. This was the mission of Jesus. Now, it is also the mission Jesus expects for the disciples, the readers of the Gospel, and Christians today who have the Holy Spirit.

8

Another Proposal for John's Pneumatology

THE SPIRIT IN JOHN's Gospel challenges the realities, relationships, and ideologies of race in the ancient world. We may assume that the main characterization of the Holy Spirit in John's Gospel solely emerges from the images of the Paraclete in John 13–16, but this is not true. What I have done within this book is to present another perspective and demonstrate that the portrayal of the Holy Spirit within the life of Jesus challenges notions of belonging and identity. I am not the only one discussing this topic; other scholars have been looking at the role of race in the construction of the Christian identity.[1] However, this study differs from other books on the Holy Spirit in John's Gospel because I bring the role of race to the forefront of our analysis. As I believe, the Gospel has a racial agenda that is intrinsically linked to its articulation and description of the Spirit. We cannot recognize these aspects without careful attention to the elements of racial difference, racial rhetoric, and the racial ideologies of the Greco-Roman world. These elements ought to influence our reading of the Spirit discourses in John's Gospel.

Why such a concern with race and identity in our study of the Spirit? There are personal biographical reasons why I engaged

1. Ok, *Constructing Ethnic Identity*; Sechrest, *Race & Rhyme*.

in such study. However, when I think about the ancient world—those people who lived long ago—I cannot assume that they had neutral and nonracial identities. Failing to consider the dynamics of race in the ancient world not only assumes that an unexamined racial identity does not matter but inadvertently supposes that the racial identity of the readers and narrative characters within the biblical text are irrelevant to the study of people in the ancient world. In fact, we do know that our interpretations of the Bible are influenced by our own subjectivity. Regardless of how hard we try to read the Bible without influences or biases, there is no such thing as an objective or neutral interpreter of the Bible.[2] Pentecostal scholars have alerted us to the role that our communities have in our understanding and interpretation of the biblical text.[3] I continue this motif but with a different focus on what we mean by "community" in that it includes the dynamics of racial identity.

Now, simply by being a Christian does not mean that we have eradicated our racial or cultural identity and assumed a theological identity. Doing so would involve only self-deception. Even more, when we think about how the readers of John's Gospel would have heard the message of Jesus, we cannot fail to be sensitive to their contextual realities. The readers of this Gospel were people who lived in a flesh-and-blood context. This also suggests that how we think about the readers of the Gospel will influence and shape how we interpret the role and function of the Holy Spirit. Having a racial consciousness in our reading of Scripture challenges us to reimagine how the Spirit was heard and understood by Jews, Greeks, and Samaritans. It urges us to rethink the situation of John's community from a racial vantage point. As such, in our analysis of the Gospel's background we affirm that the Gospel was composed for a community that included members from diverse racial backgrounds. The Gospel has a particular awareness of the multiethnic identity of the Johannine community and deliberately

---

2. For an analysis of the ethnic identity in theological hermeneutics, see Estrada, "Contextualized Hermeneutic."

3. Thomas, "Women, Pentecostals and Bible," 50; Archer, *Pentecostal Hermeneutic*, 213.

retells Jesus's ministry by including a distinct portrayal of the Spirit that would resonate with these readers.

These dynamics within the Gospel and reality of the Johannine community also oblige us to explore how racial identity and relations were understood in the Greco-Roman world. However, our concern is not anachronistic. These readers of John's Gospel heard the message of Jesus as people who lived within their own racial environment. A concern for racial identity and navigating race relations was a part of the social fabric of the Greco-Roman world. Ancient environmental theories promoted the ideas that southerners were physically too weak to rebel and northerners were incapable of devising schemes to be victorious in battle. It was assumed that the moderate climate and geographical location of Rome and Greece were the aptest environments for producing the world's most superior people. Other prevailing views on race assumed that esteemed ancestors and lineage purity were deemed more superior to those who had questionable backgrounds. Immigration and the mingling of different racial groups were expected to inevitably develop inferior kin. The pedigree of one's origin was of prime importance, and having a mixed lineage was not well esteemed in the ancient world. Lineage purity and its preservation thus defined, proclaimed, and regulated how people would relate to others.

The first-century readers of John's Gospel knew of these racial ideologies. The question is, what did they do about these racial ideologies as members of the Christian community in Ephesus? Did they allow it to influence their views of the Jewish people, Samaritans, or Greeks within their midst? Did they hold onto racial hostilities toward their fellow members within the community? I do not assume that the readers of the Gospel would have failed to notice the racial language and rhetoric within John's Gospel. Incorporating the racial rhetoric of the Greco-Roman world, including its positive and negative views of race relations, provides us with the opportunity to hear what the Spirit is saying to John's community. We recognize that the Gospel is not simply retelling

Jesus's life and ministry; it is also forging a new understanding of the Spirit in the midst of a racially diverse context and world.

RACE, THE SPIRIT, AND THE PEOPLE OF GOD IN JOHN

What have we learned thus far about John's view of the Holy Spirit in light of the racial dynamics and realities of the ancient world? To briefly review, when we explore the Spirit within Jesus's public ministry, the conversation between Jesus and Nicodemus focuses on the entrance requirements for the kingdom of God. Jesus challenges the privileges that come with being born into a Jewish ancestry. He informs Nicodemus and his Pharisaic community that a Jewish genealogical pedigree no longer provides greater access or privileged rights as children of God. Those who have difficulties in opening the boundaries for converts or proselytes are put on notice. The Spirit is the one who verifies and maternally incorporates people into the family of God. All racial lineages, as a result, are destabilized. Questionable ancestry is made insignificant, and race relations are brought closer together as a result of the common birthing experience of the Spirit. It is now the Spirit who gives birth to all the children of God.

Although Jesus's inaugurated mission to redeem the world has commenced, this still does not mean that the issues between racial groups have been resolved. If we can imagine for a moment the response of believers within John's church, they, too, are being made aware of the significance or insignificance of their respected ancestries. They no longer need to discriminate one another, view each other as second-class converts, or suspect that a non-Jewish member of the community does not have the same status as a Jewish person who claims to be a child of God. The Spirit's birthing activity repudiates all attitudes of racial superiority and rebukes those who frown upon others for having interracial marriages. All people who believe in Jesus are bonded to one another as believers through a common birthing experience of the Spirit. Anyone who doubts or prohibits the incorporation of the racially other calls into question their own born-again experience in the Spirit. In fact, they reveal that they still hold onto the presumption that racial identity alone is the defining marker that incorporates one into the family of God, and by doing so, they attest that they are not truly born of the Spirit nor know of anything related to the Spirit's maternal activity in granting rights to new members.

Yet this new birthing experience that bonds people together and eschews ancestral pedigrees does not mean that the deep historical tensions between people have been dissolved. In Jesus's journey through Samaria in John 4, the memory of racial tension between Jews and Samaritans follows. A Samaritan woman confronts Jesus on the topic of worship that was a serious issue between Jews and Samaritans. Jesus's response to her points to the worship that God seeks, one that goes beyond what is done in temple complexes, ancestral mountains, and performed by people with pure racial lineages. Jesus envisions a new future when all people, regardless of race, will inhabit the same space of worship through the Spirit. No longer is lineage purity, or the lack thereof, going to be the arbiter in determining who can or cannot worship God. To use racial identity, a focal point of segregation between Jews and Samaritans, as a means to justify the oppression and rejection of the worshiper is contrary to the presence of the Spirit.

Questions of proper worship are perhaps a concern for those who come from a Samaritan or Jewish background and reside within John's community. They, too, are being taught that worshipers of the Father can never utilize lineage purity to justify violence against sacred spaces. Although ancestral temples are no longer useful and distant, John teaches that the Spirit occupies the worshiping space of the community. In fact, to worship in the Spirit is to participate in a Spirit-inhabited space that eschews violence and attitudes of racial superiority. The Spirit indiscriminately inhabits the space of the worshiping community and expects nothing less for the people of God. Although temples are gone, the symbols of racial segregation should not be found or preserved by John's community. Even more, the Father seeks worshipers who can worship together, racially united and without hostility, in their union with and in the Spirit.

Then, in John 7, we find something different. Jesus journeys from Galilee to the Jerusalem temple during the most festive occasion, when the people reenact the wilderness experience. This journey, however, means Jesus putting his life at risk. The Jews are seeking to kill him, officers want to arrest him, the crowds desire to apprehend him, but Jesus still appears in the temple. While experiencing resistance from everyone, Jesus informs them that he will soon be departing. The Jerusalem Jews hear this and believe he is going to the Greeks. This accusation of fleeing to the Greeks is not an embarrassment. Jesus does not seek to clarify the record. Instead, under the suspicion of racial outreach, he makes it evident that he indeed is open to receiving any person. So, he stands in the temple and invites anyone to partake of the Spirit, those who are thirsty and desire living water. How many respond to Jesus's invitation is not revealed, but the writer states that the water Jesus provides is to be understood in terms of the Spirit. In a prelude to the giving of the Spirit in John 20, we see Jesus standing in the temple inviting all people to drink from him and partake of the Spirit.

Jesus, the one rejected by his own family and people, stands in the Jerusalem temple and dares all who hear his voice to receive the Spirit. As he cries out, the readers hear Jesus's invitation as well. It is the Greek audience within John's community who becomes acutely aware of Jesus's invitation. They hear within Jesus's words the refreshing invitation to partake of the Spirit in light of their experiences in the diaspora regions. Unlike the other people within John's Gospel story, they recognize the availability of the Spirit to all who believe in him. No amount of cultural suspicion or racial hostility can silence Jesus from speaking to the audience and inviting them to partake of the Spirit.

When we turn to the Farewell Discourse in John 13–16, the presence and activity of the Spirit-Paraclete are clothed in familial language. Jesus's pending death and absence from the disciples may appear to leave the disciples orphaned and in a disadvantaged

The Spirit in John's Gospel

situation with their family relations. However, the Paraclete is promised to be with them as the newly begotten community. The presence of the Paraclete binds together all people from a variety of backgrounds into one household as children of God. They are not orphaned from their families or communities. They are neither fatherless nor left in the world vulnerable, without a defender. As divinely birthed children who have the Paraclete within them, they have a new family and a new sense of understanding themselves and one another. To outsiders, they may appear as orphans without Jesus, but to one another, they are children of Jesus's family, children born of God and of the Spirit. Understanding the familial implications of the "orphan" and "children" language within John 13–16 explains not only how the members within the community would define themselves but also explains how the presence of the Paraclete sustains and unites all people into the family of God.

As a newly created community of the Spirit, this does not mean they will be free from violence and oppression. They should not only expect it, but some members of John's church are also perhaps undergoing these experiences and in fear of synagogue expulsion. Jesus's statement in 15:26–27 and 16:7–15 thus affirms that the Spirit-Paraclete will engage in communicatory and forensic activities. The Paraclete is promised to defend the disciples, those oppressed and rejected, the orphaned people of God. The hostility that the disciples and Johannine community are expected to experience (and perhaps already experiencing) includes violence in the synagogues, violence at the hands of the Roman Empire, and violence from their own families. As such, the Paraclete is promised to come to their aid and not leave them as victims or voiceless. This also means that resistance toward injustice and oppression is engaging in the ministry of the Spirit-Paraclete.

Finally, the invitation to receive the Spirit in John 20 leaves open the expectation for the disciples and believers of the gospel to continue the mission of Jesus in the world. However, John's Gospel includes the fact that the disciples were afraid and had a "fear of the Jews" after the death of Jesus. This is striking, given that they, too, are Jews. But Jesus nonetheless appears to the disciples who were hidden in a room behind locked doors on several occasions. This fear of "the Jews" perhaps genuinely reflects the readers' fear of the other—especially since many of them were from different communities and backgrounds. We do know, though, that the readers lived in a multiracial world that was both hostile and hospitable. Xenophobia and xenophilia were prominent throughout the Roman world. Nonetheless, how can they move beyond their fear of experiencing the same thing Jesus experienced? What can push them into journeying to different parts of the Roman Empire as carriers of the gospel message? Overcoming the fear of the "other" can be achieved only by breathing in the Holy Spirit. To faithfully execute Jesus's commission, the disciples and readers of the Gospel need to receive the Spirit.

This giving of the Spirit is the Gospel's own particular "Johannine Pentecost" but without the physical manifestations as we find in Acts 2. This is not to suppose that, for John's Gospel, the outward manifestations of the Spirit were irrelevant. On the contrary, the outward manifestation of the Spirit is found in the disciples' incarnational movement to the world. What truly demonstrates that the disciples have received the Spirit is if they proclaim the gospel, journey to the other, and overcome their fear of the other.

THE RACIAL SPIRIT FOR TODAY

What new insights have we gained after exploring the Spirit in light of the racial ideologies of the Greco-Roman world? I have sought to demonstrate the point that to fully understand John's view of the Spirit, we must understand the ideologies of race in the Greco-Roman world. If anything, we must realize that the Spirit as the divine presence of God addresses the challenges that result in having racialized bodies. Racial identity matters in our exegesis because the Gospel was written in such a way that it addresses the real issues and challenges of the readers, who lived in a multicultural and multiracial world. This articulation of the Spirit was needed for a community who might have had questions about differences and belonging as they participated in Jesus's mission and engaged others, those within and outside the community. The Spirit speaks to our identities, rebukes our prejudices, and reveals the insufficiency that racial ideologies and stereotypes have in the formation of a new community of believers. The Spirit is the divine wind of God who gives birth to all ethnic bodies for the purpose of gathering and forming a new community. Thus, to understand our role, identity, and relationship with others as Spirit-filled believers also means that we must confront the vicious and inhumane ideologies that have sought to divide and rank us.

As the emerging Christian community expanded and traveled into various regions, they, too, needed to deal with these issues of racial inclusion and race relations. John provides a pneumatic solution in navigating the challenges of racial inclusion and division. As readers of John's Gospel today, we, too, are reminded what it means for the Spirit to participate, dwell, and live among the communal life of believers who come from diverse racial backgrounds. The Spirit does not differentiate, discriminate, or divide the family of God. The Spirit gives birth to anyone who believes. The Spirit fills the bodies of anyone who dares to approach Jesus. To participate in the mission of the Spirit, be born of the Spirit, worship in the Spirit, derive life from the Spirit, and drink from the wells of the Spirit means that one cannot participate in practices that dehumanize, divide, and destroy racialized bodies. As such, to be a member of John's community, or any member within the early Christian community in the Greco-Roman world, means that one must denounce these dehumanizing ideologies that would prevent one from being bound together and unified as children of God born of the Spirit.

Here is the clear point of the matter: racism and dehumanizing ideologies are not simply wrong based solely on moral grounds. They are activities that run counter to the life-giving presence and family-forming movement of the Spirit. Racism and dehumanizing ideologies are by definition anti-pneumatic. That is, they are the diabolical work that dehumanizes, divides, and sets up systems of privilege and pedigree. They are activities and ideologies that run contrary to the inclusive, all-embracing, far-reaching, and life-breathing movement of the Spirit. This also leads us to wonder, can one be "born again" and claim to be a Christian while still holding onto prejudices and ideologies of racial superiority? Can one claim to be a Christian and continue to support, champion, and celebrate alongside demagogues or politicians who utilize ideologies that foment fear of the other? As I hope this monograph has answered, to do so would be to work against the Holy Spirit.

Bibliography

Abramowitz, Jonathan S., and Shannon M. Blakey. "Overestimation of Threat." In *Clinical Handbook of Fear and Anxiety: Maintenance Processes and Treatment Mechanisms*, edited by Jonathan S. Abramowitz and Shannon M. Blakey, 7–25. Washington, DC: American Psychological Association, 2020.
Allison, Dale C., Jr. *Resurrecting Jesus: The Earliest Christian Tradition and Its Interpreters*. London: T&T Clark, 2005.
Anderson, Allan Heaton. *Introduction to Pentecostalism: Global Charismatic Christianity*. Introduction to Religion. New York: Cambridge University Press, 2004.
Anderson, Robert T., and Terry Giles. *The Keepers: An Introduction to the History and Culture of Samaritans*. Peabody, MA: Hendrickson, 2002.
Archer, Kenneth J. *A Pentecostal Hermeneutic: Spirit, Scripture, and Community*. Cleveland, TN: CPT, 2009.
Aristotle. *Politics*. Translated by H. Rackham. LCL 264. Cambridge, MA: Harvard University Press, 1932.
Ashton, John. *Understanding the Fourth Gospel*. 2nd ed. New York: Oxford, 2008.
Balsdon, J. P. V. D. *Romans and Aliens*. London: Duckworth, 1979.
Barrett, C. K. *The Gospel According to St. John: An Introduction with Commentary and Notes on the Greek Text*. London: Camelot, 1970.
———. "Holy Spirit in the Fourth Gospel." *JTS* 1 (1950) 1–15.
Bauckham, Richard, ed. *The Gospels for All Christians: Rethinking the Gospel Audiences*. New Testament Studies. Grand Rapids: Eerdmans, 1998.
———. *The Testimony of the Beloved Disciple: Narrative, History, and Theology in the Gospel of John*. Grand Rapids: Baker Academic, 2007.
Beasley-Murray, George. *John*. WBC 36. Nashville: Nelson, 1999.
Belleville, Linda. "Born of Water and Spirit: John 3:5." *TJ* 1 (1980) 125–41.
Betz, O. *Der Paraklet: Fürsprecher im häretischen Spätjudentum, im Johannes-Evangelium und in neu gefundenen gnostischen Schriften*. AGJU. Leiden: Brill, 1963.
Blomberg, Craig L. *The Historical Reliability of John's Gospel: Issues and Commentary*. Downers Grove, IL: IVP Academic, 2001.

Bibliography

Bowman, John. *The Samaritan Problem: Studies in the Relationships of Samaritanism, Judaism, and Early Christianity.* Pittsburgh Theological Monograph 4. Eugene, OR: Pickwick, 1975.

Brown, Raymond E. *Community of the Beloved Disciple: The Life, Loves, and Hates of an Individual Church in New Testament Times.* New York: Paulist, 1979.

———. *The Gospel According to John.* 2 vols. AB 29-29A. Garden City, NY: Doubleday, 1966, 1978.

———. *An Introduction to the Gospel of John.* Edited by Francis J. Moloney. AYBRL. New York: Doubleday, 2003.

Brown, Tricia Gates. *Spirit in the Writings of John: Johannine Pneumatology in Social-Scientific Perspective.* JSNTSup. London: T&T Clark, 2003.

Buell, Denise Kimber. "Challenges and Strategies for Speaking About Ethnicity in the New Testament and New Testament Studies." *Svensk Exegetisk Arsbok* 79 (2014) 33-51.

———. *Why This New Race: Ethnic Reasoning in Early Christianity.* Gender, Theory, and Religion. New York: Columbia University Press, 2007.

Buell, Denise Kimber, and Caroline Hodge. "The Politics of Interpretation: The Rhetoric of Race and Ethnicity in Paul." *JBL* 123 (2004) 235-51.

Bultmann, Rudolf. *The Gospel of John: A Commentary.* Philadelphia: John Knox, 1971.

Burge, Gary M. *The Anointed Community: The Holy Spirit in the Johannine Tradition.* Grand Rapids: Eerdmans, 1987.

Cicero. *On Duties.* Translated by Walter Miller. LCL 30. Cambridge, MA: Harvard University Press, 1913.

———. *On the Republic. On the Laws.* Translated by Clinton W. Keyes. LCL 213. Cambridge, MA: Harvard University Press, 1928.

Cohen, Shaye J. D. *The Beginnings of Jewishness: Boundaries, Varieties, Uncertainties.* HCS. Berkeley: University of California Press, 1999.

Collins, John J. *Between Athens and Jerusalem: Jewish Identity in the Hellenistic Diaspora.* Biblical Resource. Grand Rapids: Eerdmans, 2000.

Cotton, Hannah M., et al., eds. *Jerusalem: Part 1, 1-704.* Vol. 1 of *Corpus Inscriptionum Iudaeae/Palaestinae.* New York: De Gruyter, 2011.

Culpepper, R. Alan. *Anatomy of the Fourth Gospel: A Study in Literary Design.* Philadelphia: Fortress, 1987.

Diodorus Siculus. *Library of History, Volume 8: Books 16.66—17.* Translated by C. Bradford Welles. LCL 422. Cambridge, MA: Harvard University Press, 1963.

Dionysius of Halicarnassus. *Roman Antiquities, Volume 1: Books 1-2.* Translated by Earnest Cary. LCL 319. Cambridge, MA: Harvard University Press, 1937.

———. *Library of History, Volume 12: Fragments of Books 33-40.* Translated by Francis R. Walton. LCL 423. Cambridge, MA: Harvard University Press, 1967.

Bibliography

Dodd, C. H. *The Interpretation of the Fourth Gospel.* New York: Cambridge University Press, 1970.
Edelman, Diana. "Ethnicity and Early Israel." In *Ethnicity and the Bible*, edited by Mark G. Brett, 25–55. BibInt 9. London: Brill, 1996.
Eslinger, Lyle. "The Wooing of the Woman at the Well: Jesus, the Reader, and Reader-Response Criticism." In *The Gospel of John as Literature: An Anthology of Twentieth-Century Perspectives*, edited by Mark W. G. Stibbe, 165–82. NTTS. Leiden: Brill, 1993.
Espinosa, Gastón. *William J. Seymour and the Origins of Global Pentecostalism: A Biography & Documentary History.* Durham, NC: Duke University Press, 2014.
Estrada, Rodolfo Galvan, III. "Is a Contextualized Hermeneutic the Future of Pentecostal Readings? The Implications of a Pentecostal Hermeneutic for a Chicano/Latino Community." *Pneuma* 37 (2015) 341–55.
———. *A Latino Reading of Race, Kinship, and the Empire: John's Prologue.* Cham, Switz.: Palgrave MacMillan, 2023.
———. *A Pneumatology of Race in the Gospel of John: An Ethnocritical Study.* Eugene, OR: Pickwick, 2019.
———. "The Racial Significance of Paul's Clothing Metaphor (Romans 13:14; Galatians 3:27; Ephesians 4:24; Colossians 3:10)." *Religions* 14 (2023) 1–13.
———. "The Spirit as an Inner Witness in John 15.26." *Journal of Pentecostal Theology* 22 (2013) 77–94.
———. "What Does the Paraclete Have to Do with Dreamers? A Pneumatological Paradigm for Latino/a Social-Political Advocacy." *Perspectivas* 19 (2019) 67–81.
Fitzgerald, J. T. "Orphans in Mediterranean Antiquity and Early Christianity." *AcT* 23 (2016) 29–48.
Florus. *Epitome of Roman History.* Translated by E. S. Forster. LCL 231. Cambridge, MA: Harvard University Press, 1929.
Fuglseth, Kåre Sigvald. *Johannine Sectarianism in Perspective: A Sociological, Historical, and Comparative Analysis of Temple and Social Relationships in the Gospel of John, Philo, and Qumran.* NovTSup 119. Leiden: Brill, 2005.
Grese, William. "'Unless One is Born Again': The Use of a Heavenly Journey in John 3." *JBL* 107 (1988) 677–93.
Grigsby, Bruce. "'If Any Man Thirsts . . .': Observations on the Rabbinic Background of John 7:37–39." *Bib* 67 (1986) 101–8.
Gruen, Erich S. *Rethinking the Other in Antiquity.* Martin Classical Lectures. Princeton, NJ: Princeton University Press, 2011.
Hall, Edith. *Inventing the Barbarian: Greek Self-Definition Through Tragedy.* Oxford Classical Monographs. New York: Oxford University Press, 2004.
Hall, Jonathan M. *Ethnic Identity in Greek Antiquity.* New York: Cambridge University Press, 2000.
———. *Hellenicity: Between Ethnicity and Culture.* Chicago: University of Chicago Press, 2002.

Bibliography

Hanson, K. C. "All in the Family: Kinship in Agrarian Roman Palestine." In *The Social World of the New Testament: Insights and Models*, edited by Jerome H. Neyrey and Eric C. Stewart, 26–46. Peabody, MA: Hendrickson, 2008.

Herodotus. *The Persian Wars: Books 1–2*. Translated by A. D. Godley. LCL 117. Cambridge, MA: Harvard University Press, 1920.

Hippocrates. *Ancient Medicine. Airs, Waters, Places. Epidemics 1 and 3. The Oath. Precepts. Nutriment*. Edited and translated by Paul Potter. LCL 147. Cambridge, MA: Harvard University Press, 2022.

Hodge, Caroline Johnson. *If Sons, Then Heirs: A Study of Kinship and Ethnicity in the Letters of Paul*. New York: Oxford University Press, 2007.

Homer. *Iliad*. Translated by A. T. Murray. Revised by William F. Wyatt. 2 vols. LCL 170–71. Cambridge, MA: Harvard University Press, 1924, 1925.

Horrell, David. "Race, Nation, People: Ethnic Identity-Construction in 1 Peter 2:9." *NTS* 58 (2012) 123–43.

Hübner, Sabine R. "Callirhoe's Dilemma: Remarriage and Stepfathers in the Greco-Roman East." In *Growing Up Fatherless in Antiquity*, edited by Sabine R. Hübner and David M. Ratzan, 61–82. New York: Cambridge University Press, 2009.

———. "Fatherless Antiquity? Perspectives on 'Fatherlessness' in the Ancient Mediterranean." In *Growing Up Fatherless in Antiquity*, edited by Sabine R. Hübner and David M. Ratzan, 3–28. New York: Cambridge University Press, 2009.

Hwa-Froelich, Deborah A. *Social Communication Development and Disorders*. 2nd ed. Language and Speech Disorders. Milton: Taylor & Francis, 2022.

Irenaeus of Lyons. *Adversus haereses*. In *The Ante-Nicene Fathers*, edited by Alexander Roberts et al., 1:309–567. Buffalo, NY: Christian Literature, 1885.

Isaac, Benjamin. *The Invention of Racism in Classical Antiquity*. Race, Justice & Equity. Princeton, NJ: Princeton University Press, 2004.

Isocrates. *To Demonicus. To Nicocles. Nicocles or the Cyprians. Panegyricus. To Philip. Archidamus*. Translated by George Norlin. LCL 209. Cambridge, MA: Harvard University Press, 1928.

Johnston, George. *The Spirit-Paraclete in the Gospel of John*. SNTSMS 12. New York: Cambridge University Press, 1970.

Josephus. *Jewish Antiquities, Volume 1: Books 1–3*. Translated by H. St. J. Thackeray. LCL 242. Cambridge, MA: Harvard University Press, 1930.

———. *Jewish Antiquities, Volume 2: Books 4–6*. Translated by H. St. J. Thackeray and Ralph Marcus. LCL 490. Cambridge, MA: Harvard University Press, 1930.

———. *Jewish Antiquities, Volume 3: Books 7–8*. Translated by Ralph Marcus. LCL 281. Cambridge, MA: Harvard University Press, 1934.

———. *Jewish Antiquities, Volume 4: Books 9–11*. Translated by Ralph Marcus. LCL 326. Cambridge, MA: Harvard University Press, 1937.

———. *Jewish Antiquities, Volume 5: Books 12–13*. Translated by Ralph Marcus. LCL 365. Cambridge, MA: Harvard University Press, 1943.

Bibliography

———. *Jewish Antiquities, Volume 6: Books 14–15*. Translated by Ralph Marcus and Allen Wikgren. LCL 489. Cambridge, MA: Harvard University Press, 1943.
———. *Jewish Antiquities, Volume 7: Books 16–17*. Translated by Ralph Marcus and Allen Wikgren. LCL 410. Cambridge, MA: Harvard University Press, 1963.
———. *Jewish Antiquities, Volume 8: Books 18–19*. Translated by Louis H. Feldman. LCL 433. Cambridge, MA: Harvard University Press, 1965.
———. *Jewish Antiquities, Volume 9: Book 20*. Translated by Louis H. Feldman. LCL 456. Cambridge, MA: Harvard University Press, 1965.
———. *The Jewish War, Volume 1: Books 1–2*. Translated by H. St. J. Thackeray. LCL 203. Cambridge, MA: Harvard University Press, 1927.
———. *The Jewish War, Volume 3: Books 5–7*. Translated by H. St. J. Thackeray. LCL 210. Cambridge, MA: Harvard University Press, 1928.
———. *The Life. Against Apion*. Translated by H. St. J. Thackeray. LCL 186. Cambridge, MA: Harvard University Press, 1926.
Keener, Craig S. *The Gospel of John: A Commentary*. 2 vols. Grand Rapids: Baker Academic, 2003.
———. *The Spirit in the Gospels and Acts: Divine Purity and Power*. Peabody, MA: Hendrickson, 1997.
Kim, Jean. "Korean Feminist Reading of John 4:1–42." *Semeia* 78 (1997) 109–19.
Knoppers, Gary N. *Jews and the Samaritans: The Origins and History of Their Early Relations*. New York: Oxford University Press, 2013.
Koester, Craig R. *The Word of Life: A Theology of John's Gospel*. Grand Rapids: Eerdmans, 2008.
Köstenberger, Andreas J. *A Theology of John's Gospel and Letters*. Biblical Theology of the New Testament. Grand Rapids: Zondervan Academic, 2009.
Köstenberger, Andreas J., and Scott Swain. *Father, Son, and Spirit: The Trinity and John's Gospel*. Edited by D. A. Carson. New Studies in Biblical Theology. Downers Grove, IL: IVP Academic, 2008.
Lindars, Barnabas. *The Gospel of John*. NCB. London: Oliphants, 1972.
Loader, William. *Jesus in John's Gospel: Structure and Issues in Johannine Christology*. Grand Rapids: Eerdmans, 2017.
Marcus, Joel. "Johannine Christians and Baptist Sectarians within Late First-Century Judaism." In *John and Judaism: A Contested Relationship in Context*, edited by R. Alan Culpepper and Paul Anderson, 155–63. RBS 87. Atlanta: SBL, 2017.
Martyn, J. Louis. *History and Theology in the Fourth Gospel*. 3rd ed. NTL. Louisville: Westminster, 2003.
McCoskey, Denise Eileen. *Race: Antiquity and Its Legacy*. Ancients & Moderns. New York: Oxford University Press, 2012.
McKnight, Scot. *A Light Among the Gentiles: Jewish Missionary Activity in the Second Temple Period*. Minneapolis: Fortress, 1991.

Bibliography

Meeks, Wayne A. "The Man from Heaven in Johannine Sectarianism." In *In Search of the Early Christians: Selected Essays*, edited by Allen R. Hilton and H. Gregory Snyder, 55–90. New Haven, CT: Yale University Press, 2002.

———. *The Prophet-King: Moses Tradition and the Johannine Christology.* Johannine Monograph Series. Eugene, OR: Wipf and Stock, 2017.

Menken, Maarten. "'Born of God' or 'Begotten by God'? A Translation Problem in the Johannine Writings." *NovT* 51 (2009) 352–68.

———. "The Origin of the Old Testament Quotation in John 7:38." *NovT* 38 (1996) 160–75.

Metzger, Bruce Manning. *The Text of the New Testament: Its Transmission, Corruption, and Restoration.* 2nd ed. New York: Oxford University Press, 1968.

———. *A Textual Commentary on the Greek New Testament: A Companion Volume to the United Bible Societies' Greek New Testament (Third Edition).* London: United Bible Societies, 1971.

Millos, Samuel Pérez. *Juan: Commentario Exegético al Texto Greiego del Nuevo Testamento.* Barcelona: Clie, 2016.

Moloney, Francis J. *The Resurrection of the Messiah: A Narrative Commentary on the Resurrection Accounts in the Four Gospels.* New York: Paulist, 2013.

Morris, Leon. *The Gospel According to John.* NICNT. Grand Rapids: Eerdmans, 1995.

O'Day, Gail R. *Revelation in the Fourth Gospel: Narrative Mode and Theological Claim.* Minneapolis: Fortress, 1986.

Ok, Janette H. *Constructing Ethnic Identity in 1 Peter: Who You Are No Longer.* London: T&T Clark, 2021.

Orian, Matan. "The Purpose of the Balustrade in the Herodian Temple." *JSJ* 51 (2020) 487–524.

Philo. *On the Cherubim. The Sacrifices of Abel and Cain. The Worse Attacks the Better. On the Posterity and Exile of Cain. On the Giants.* Translated by F. H. Colson and G. H. Whitaker. LCL 227. Cambridge, MA: Harvard University Press, 1929.

———. *On the Embassy to Gaius. General Indexes.* Translated by F. H. Colson. Index by J. W. Earp. LCL 379. Cambridge, MA: Harvard University Press, 1962.

———. *On the Special Laws, Book 4. On the Virtues. On Rewards and Punishments.* Translated by F. H. Colson. LCL 341. Cambridge, MA: Harvard University Press, 1939.

Plato. *Euthyphro. Apology. Crito. Phaedo.* Edited and translated by Christopher Emlyn-Jones and William Preddy. LCL 36. Cambridge, MA: Harvard University Press, 2017.

———. *Statesman. Philebus. Ion.* Translated by Harold North Fowler and W. R. M. Lamb. LCL 164. Cambridge, MA: Harvard University Press, 1925.

———. *Timaeus. Critias. Cleitophon. Menexenus. Epistles.* Translated by R. G. Bury. LCL 234. Cambridge, MA: Harvard University Press, 1929.

Bibliography

Pliny. *Natural History, Volume 1: Books 1-2.* Translated by H. Rackham. LCL 330. Cambridge, MA: Harvard University Press, 1938.

———. *Natural History, Volume 2: Books 3-7.* Translated by H. Rackham. LCL 352. Cambridge, MA: Harvard University Press, 1942.

Plutarch. *Demosthenes and Cicero. Alexander and Caesar.* Translated by Bernadotte Perrin. Vol. 7 of *Lives.* LCL 99. Cambridge, MA: Harvard University Press, 1919.

Porphyry. "On Abstinence from Animal Food." In *Jewish Life and Thought Among Greeks and Romans: Primary Readings,* edited by Louis H. Feldman and Meyer Reinhold, 7. Minneapolis: Fortress, 1996.

Porsch, Felix. *Pneuma und Wort: Ein exegetischer Beitrag zur Pneumatologie des Johannesevangeliums.* Frankfurter Theologische Studien 16. Frankfurt: Knecht, 1974.

Ptolemy. *Tetrabiblos.* Translated by F. E. Robbins. LCL 435. Cambridge, MA: Harvard University Press, 1940.

Rahim, Muddathir Abdel, et al. "UNESCO Statement on Race and Racial Prejudice." *Current Anthropology* 9 (1968) 270-72.

Reinhartz, Adele. "'And the Word Was Begotten': Divine Epigenesis in the Gospel of John." *Semeia* 85 (1999) 83-103.

Rendtorff, Rolf. "The Gēr in the Priestly Laws of the Pentateuch." In *Ethnicity and the Bible,* edited by Mark G. Brett, 77-87. BibInt 9. London: Brill, 1996.

Sanders, E. P. *The Historical Figure of Jesus.* New York: Penguin, 1995.

Schäfer, Peter. *Judeophobia: Attitudes Toward the Jews in the Ancient World.* Cambridge, MA: Harvard University Press, 1998.

Scheidel, Walter. "The Demographic Background." In *Growing Up Fatherless in Antiquity,* edited by Sabine R. Hübner and David M. Ratzan, 31-40. New York: Cambridge University Press, 2009.

Schneiders, Sandra M. "Born Anew." *ThTo* 44 (1987) 189-96.

———. *The Revelatory Text: Interpreting the New Testament as Sacred Scripture.* Wilmington, DE: Glazier, 1991.

Sechrest, Love L. *A Former Jew: Paul and the Dialectics of Race.* LNTS. New York: Bloomsbury, 2009.

———. *Race & Rhyme: Rereading the New Testament.* Grand Rapids: Eerdmans, 2022.

Segovia, Fernando F. *The Farewell of the Word: The Johannine Call to Abide.* Minneapolis: Fortress, 1991.

———. "The Journey(s) of the Word of God: A Reading of the Plot of the Fourth Gospel." *Semeia* 53 (1991) 23-54.

Sheridan, Ruth. "The Paraclete as Successor in the Johannine Farewell Discourse: A Comparative Literary Analysis." *Australian eJournal of Theology* 18 (2011) 129-40.

Sherwin-White, Adrian. *Racial Prejudice in Imperial Rome.* New York: Cambridge University Press, 1970.

Bibliography

Sigismund, Marcus. "'Without Father, Without Mother, Without Genealogy': Fatherlessness in the Old and New Testament." In *Growing Up Fatherless in Antiquity*, edited by Sabine R. Hübner and David M. Ratzan, 83–102. New York: Cambridge University Press, 2009.

Skinner, Christopher W. *Reading John*. Cascade Companions. Eugene, OR: Cascade, 2015.

Smalley, Stephen. "The Paraclete: Pneumatology in the Johannine Gospel and Apocalypse." In *Exploring the Gospel of John: In Honor of D. Moody Smith*, edited by R. Alan Culpepper and C. Clifton Black, 289–300. Louisville: Westminster John Knox, 1996.

Smith, D. Moody. *John Among the Gospels*. Columbia: University of South Carolina Press, 2001.

Stube, John Carlson. *A Graeco-Roman Rhetorical Reading of the Farewell Discourse*. LNTS. London: T&T Clark, 2006.

Suetonius. *Julius. Augustus. Tiberius. Gaius Caligula*. Translated by J. C. Rolfe. Introduction by K. R. Bradley. Vol. 1 of *Lives of the Caesars*. LCL 31. Cambridge, MA: Harvard University Press, 1914.

Thomas, John Christopher. *Spirit of the New Testament*. Dorset, UK: Deo, 2005.

———. "Women, Pentecostals and the Bible: An Experiment in Pentecostal Hermeneutics." *Journal of Pentecostal Theology* 5 (1994) 41–56.

Thompson, Marianne Meye. *The God of the Gospel of John*. Grand Rapids: Eerdmans, 2001.

———. *John: A Commentary*. NTL. Louisville: Westminster John Knox, 2015.

Turner, Max. *The Holy Spirit and Spiritual Gifts: In the New Testament Church and Today*. Peabody, MA: Hendrickson, 2009.

UNESCO [United Nations Education, Scientific and Cultural Organization]. "The Scientific Basis for Human Unity." *UNESCO Courier* 3 (1950) 8–9.

Van Tilborg, Sjef. *Reading John in Ephesus*. NovTSup 83. Leiden: Brill, 1996.

Weissenrieder, Annette. "Spirit and Rebirth in the Gospel of John." *R&T* 21 (2014) 58–85.

Witherington, Ben, III. "The Waters of Birth: John 3.5 and 1 John 5.6–8." *NTS* 35 (1989) 155–60.

Woolf, Greg. "Becoming Roman, Staying Greek: Culture, Identity, and the Civilizing Process in the Roman East." *Proceedings of the Cambridge Philological Society* 40 (1994) 116–43.

Xenophon. *Memorabilia. Oeconomicus. Symposium. Apology*. Translated by E. C. Marchant, O. J. Todd. Revised by Jeffrey Henderson. LCL 168. Cambridge, MA: Harvard University Press, 2013.

Yong, Amos. *The Spirit Poured Out on All Flesh: Pentecostalism and the Possibility of Global Theology*. Grand Rapids: Baker Academic, 2005.

www.ingramcontent.com/pod-product-compliance
Lightning Source LLC
Chambersburg PA
CBHW020855160426
43192CB00007B/935